A GUIDE TO YOUR

MW01290953

THE ASCENSION HANDBOOK

BY THE TWO MARYS

CHANNELED BY JESSIE KEENER
INTERVIEWED/EDITED BY JOEL D. ANASTASI

FOREWORD

As a child I lived in Brazil for two years where I learned about Mother Mary from our beloved live-in servant, Rosa, a Catholic who was very devoted to the Virgin Mary. I have always been drawn to the Mary energy in times of crisis, and I find great comfort praying to her. Her unconditional love has assisted me throughout my life.

The Two Marys spontaneously began "coming through" me in early May of 2010. I was giving my dear friend and partner at The Modern Day Mystery School, Phillip Collins, a healing session, when I felt guided to hold his feet. As I centered myself with my hands on his feet, I received this extra energy that happens when I channel. I had channeled St. Francis earlier in my life and helped souls who had died cross over to the Light. So I was familiar with the experience of being a conscious channel. (I want to thank my first spiritual teacher, GK, for teaching me to use my gifts.)

As I worked with Phillip a message came through for him that I spoke out loud. The message ended with, "We are the Two Marys." That was it! I had no idea the Two Marys were Mother Mary and Mary Magdalene combining their energies. I just knew I felt this incredible ecstatic energy of love.

Phillip shared his experience with Joel, a beloved friend and master teacher who had begun teaching at our school. Because of his special connection with the Mary energy, Joel asked if I would be willing to give him a session with them. I agreed, though I had no thought regarding the *significance* of his request or what it might possibly lead to.

Joel and I began a series of conversations with the Two Marys—I channeled the Two Marys and he recorded and transcribed the sessions. The love that the Two Marys projected is indescribable. I found myself looking forward to each session to receive their energy and wisdom. In time they told us that, if we chose, we were to complete an important spiritual project called *The Ascension Handbook*.

Joel and I share a deep interest in Ascension, which is the expansion of consciousness until we reach the joyful recognition and understanding that we are God. I have been studying and teaching spiritual evolution for thirty years and cofounded a Mystery School here in Fort Lauderdale dedicated to supporting people's spiritual growth.

I feel humble and grateful to be the receiver of this information. This experience has been incredibly healing as the power of the words of the Two Marys have changed and opened me to my truth, which is, of course, divine love.

My prayer is that you too will experience that love and that your heart will be awakened and filled with the ecstasy of their compassion and grace. It is here for you. It is here for humanity.

—Jessie Keener, Fort Lauderdale, Florida, September 2011

I have always loved Mary, Mother of Jesus. I was raised in the Catholic Church where Mary is venerated. I traveled twice to Medjugorje, Yugoslavia, in the 1980s where Mary was reported to be appearing to several young people. I remember standing in an empty field outside the village under an inky black sky filled with stars imploring the Virgin Mary to heal my dearest friend and partner who was dying back home in the United States. I stood praying in silence but received no message. My partner passed away months later.

I never knew much about Mary Magdalene. My church taught she was a prostitute redeemed by Jesus. The mental image I had of Mary was of the stunning sculpture by Donatello I saw years ago in Florence, Italy. One of the first realistic sculptures of the Italian Renaissance, it depicts Mary Magdalene as a disease-ravaged hag dressed in rags.

Two decades later I find myself writing a foreword at the request of the combined energies (explained in *The Ascension Handbook*) of Mother Mary and Mary Magdalene to tell how the writing of *The Ascension Handbook* came about. I'm trying to resist that old cliché, "If someone had told me…."

This wonderful project began at lunch with Jessie Keener in spring 2010 in Fort Lauderdale, Florida. Jessie and I had been introduced by an old friend, Phillip Collins, who, with Jessie, had cofounded the Modern Day Mystery School in Fort Lauderdale. I led a book discussion group at the school on my book, *The Second Coming: The Archangel Gabriel Proclaims a New Age*. Jessie and I were becoming good friends. It didn't hurt that she loved my book. During lunch, Jessie told me that she channeled the Two Marys, the combined energies of Mother Mary and Mary Magdalene. I didn't know what that meant, but I sure wanted to find out.

My book, *The Second Coming*, records my conversations with the Archangel Gabriel channeled by trance channel Robert Baker. I had long gotten over my skepticism at the idea of channeling divine spirits, which was definitely outside of my religious schooling. I'm a trained journalist. I found channel Robert Baker completely credible and my experience with Archangel Gabriel powerful. I was ready for another divine project.

With Jessie serving as the channel, I had my first conversation with the Two Marys (that is what they said to call them) in May 2010. I was embraced by the most powerful energy of love I have ever experienced. It wasn't until March 2011 that the Two Marys revealed that our project would be "a series of intelligent articulations regarding the human conundrums with Ascension."

I had no idea what that meant, but *The Ascension Handbook* is the result. It is truly what the subtitle says, A GUIDE TO YOUR ECSTATIC UNION WITH GOD. I love the Two Marys. I love what they teach humankind about this powerful time of Ascension. I am honored that they chose to work with me. And I hope they give me another job.

—Joel Anastasi, Hoboken, New Jersey, September 2011

INTRODUCTION

Beloved students, you chose this lifetime as the culmination of all that you have ever been. You chose this lifetime whether you understand all your previous lives or not. You chose this lifetime to fully access God in your body, through your body, and into what we call the Ascension Process.

We are the Two Marys, and we have entwined our frequencies as the Two Marys in this expression for the purpose of supporting you, beloved students, in fully realizing yourselves as God. This is called the Ascension Process—ascending from a limited awareness of what it means to be alive as a human and expanding that into the understanding that, indeed, you are God.

The Two Marys are the enjoining of the Mother Mary and Mary Magdalene at a very specific frequency for the purpose of assisting humanity in Ascension. As you read these words, we invite you into this exact frequency. If you choose, give yourself permission to enter this frequency of Ascension, for you have everything to gain and nothing to lose.

What we mean by this is you have spent lifetime after lifetime striving to serve your spiritual blueprint, striving to serve your soul's desire for unity, striving to become God. And now we are here to assist. Entering this frequency means you lose nothing. It means that you are open to very specific assistance from this fifth-dimensional frequency. We wish to introduce ourselves the following way: we are the entwining of Mother Mary, the Mother of Jesus, and Mary Magdalene, the twin flame of Jesus.

Therefore, throughout this teaching the Christ Consciousness will permeate your existence, if you choose to invite this frequency. For those of you who have always resonated with the Christ Consciousness, welcome home. For those of you who find that information new, welcome. Welcome to your home. The Christ Consciousness is not about religion. It is about love. The Christ Consciousness says I am God. This is the same as all spiritual teachings. All spiritual teachings say the student is God. The exercises that have always been on your planet to assist the student in moving forward have always been for the purpose of demonstrating to the student that he is God.

All of the gurus that have ever walked on your planet, all of the avatars—whether Jesus, Buddha, Mohammed, or many others— have taught the very same thing. Welcome to your Ascension, beloved students. That is not to say you have not already been diligently ascending, for many of you have been. And because you picked up this very book, because you are reading these very words, we acknowledge you. We acknowledge that in your heart you know that you belong in Ascension, that you belong to God and God belongs to you.

We wish to impart this truth to you, beloved students: GOD IS COUNTING ON YOU TO BE GOD.

That is all and nothing more. Consider that. Take a deep breath as you read that. Imagine to yourself, "What does it really mean that God is counting on me?" God's mission, God's plan, is to fully experience. Nothing more. Nothing less. God is all that is; therefore, God's mission is your being God.

As you read the discourses that we have given you in *The Ascension Handbook,* pay attention to the part of your mind that wants to argue about whether you are God. You will be given tools, information, and wisdom, and you will be given choices. Ascension always involves choices. There are no "shoulds" in this handbook.

Our goal is to create a continuous process for you by which you can ascend. Here is the truth. You will ascend anyway. Your Ascension is guaranteed. The only question is when. If you desire Ascension NOW in your life, this is your book. If you feel that you have all the time in the world, perhaps this is not your book. For our purpose is to cocreate Ascension with each and every student.

If the cocreation of your Ascension resonates with you, it is time to begin. It is time for you to learn about Ascension in this frequency. It is time for you to get to know yourself through this material. It is time for you to increase your capacity for self-love and for joy. It is time for you to experience ecstasy that you experience only when you are fully connected to God. IT IS TIME TO RETURN TO YOUR TRUE NATURE AS GOD.

Beloved students, we acknowledge you. We are here to support you. And if you choose, we are willing to work with you directly through these materials. One note: as you read these words in these discourses, the very words themselves contain the necessary frequencies for Ascension. That is a very important distinction. It is not simply the core teachings. It is also the FREQUENCY of how the teachings are being communicated. Perhaps you will wish to read some of this out loud. Perhaps you will wish to have a group book discussion and have other members reading to each other. Perhaps you will wish to read this over and over. The frequencies will impart movement within your being. They will stir you. They will move you.

Beloved students, never underestimate the power of the words. Read slowly. Take deep breaths often. Stop when you need to stop. Rest. There is no hurry in getting through the discourses. Most of you, once you have gotten through this material, will want to keep engaging with it as long as you exist in this dimension, which we call the third dimension.

You have vast resources available to you, beloved students. As we give you this information here and now, we are sending you our greatest blessings. We are sending you frequencies to uplift you and place you directly in the center of your heart. Embrace that, beloved students. Embrace the truth:

YOU ARE GOD. YOU BELONG TO GOD.
GOD BELONGS TO YOU. WELCOME HOME!

—THE TWO MARYS

DEVELOP THE DISCIPLINE OF THE DISCIPLE

M: Greetings, beloved Joel. It is with great honor and pleasure that we entrain with you on this frequency for the unified field consciousness of Ascension. We greet you on this most auspicious day. We are here today eagerly beginning a conversation to create Ascension for those who resonate with Ascension on the human plane—Ascension from the third dimension through the fourth into the fifth dimension. We are not here to work on the fourth dimension. That is already happening, and that is not our frequency.

We are here to serve as a bridge in communication, a bridge of grace, vibration, and frequency to the fifth dimension. You have been working very diligently on yourself, beloved Joel, on your gifts and your talents, and we acknowledge this. We acknowledge that you have been picking up your pen.

We acknowledge that you are beginning to feel the change in your own frequencies as you move this energy through your body and become a conduit for it. We know that you are beginning to see the power of this for yourself. More important, you are beginning to experience the human process of going from resistance to surrender to the gifts that are not about you but are sponsored *through you.* Do you see?

J: Yes. I have a question about my reluctance to use my gifts. I guess I haven't been picking up my pen [automatic writing] to receive messages from you because, in truth, I doubted its authenticity. I didn't know if it was you or me writing the messages. I think I'm a proxy for people who don't understand that as you spend time with a spiritual gift, the gift develops. Would you explain what happens when we turn to that inner place and practice using our spiritual gifts consistently?

M: It is a most valuable question, and that is why we are leading with the topic of DISCIPLINE today. It is essential for those committed to the Ascension Process to understand that no matter what their commitment, their ego will take positions adverse to that commitment.

Much like a seedling sprouts, each human has a particular gift, a particular way that she receives spirit. For each human being it comes in primary forms of expression such as automatic writing, hearing, seeing, feeling, or knowing that these gifts are there to be tapped and utilized.

In the beginning it is called imagination, much like if one plants a seed or puts it in water to sprout. There is the potential for that life to exist beyond that form of the seed. As the environment encourages that seed to sprout, it moves from potential to being alive, but it is very fragile and delicate. What the environment does next will determine its ability to survive and thrive or to move to a different frequency, for this one is not suitable.

For humans, as they begin to allow their gifts to manifest, it is a fragile relationship. The environment surrounding that gift is paramount. When we speak of the *environment*, we are not speaking of geography or the aesthetics of a room. We are speaking of the environment of the mental body and the consciousness. These are the things that create an environment where that seedling can thrive or barely survive. So the environment will create the consciousness that allows the gift to strengthen or perish for that individual's lifetime. Of course, there is no right or wrong. You get many chances, many lifetimes, to determine for yourself, as a soul, whether or not you will create an environment in which your gift may thrive.

The discipline required is enormous. The discipline becomes everything. The purpose of discipline is to support your freedom, your freedom to be your gifts and talents. So we will be having a series of conversations in *The Ascension Handbook*, and the first one is DISCIPLINE—discipline as it pertains to spiritual growth.

We wish all who read this handbook to understand that by using discipline they become a DISCIPLE, a disciple of love, a disciple of light, and a disciple of universal law. We invite them to pick up that title, to own it, and to feel the depth and sincerity of how that resonates in their heart. For those who pick up their handbook will remember that they chose Ascension eons ago. They chose it and it is here. So the disciple surrenders consistently. HE SURRENDERS HIS EGO TO THE LARGER CONSCIOUSNESS.

In human terms this has been done over and over on your planet. Certainly, when we walked with our beloved Jesus, that was the nature of being disciples to the Christ Consciousness. So when you are a disciple, your consciousness is not yours. Your consciousness does not belong to you anymore. This is a tricky subject that most do not speak about. Most people take the information from the fifth dimension and make it small enough to fit into their little world, which includes a PRIVATE SELF and a PRIVATE CONSCIOUSNESS that belongs to them.

In reality, this is folly. For your CONSCIOUSNESS does NOT belong to you. Indeed, your SELF does NOT belong to you. This is a big part of the reason why there is so much strife and conflict on your beloved Gaia. For thousands of years, the misinterpretation of self and consciousness has been that the self is private, that, "It is mine to own, to occupy, to treat, or not to treat as a member of the universe."

As we work together, we invite you to begin to investigate and question, "Where am I still entertaining this private notion?" Begin to look at the mirrors around you. Start to notice how limiting a private self and a private consciousness truly are.

When you start to appreciate that you are far more than you ever thought you were as a private self, when you begin to realize that your consciousness is, in fact, infinite, then you begin to understand the limitations of what society has taught you to believe about yourself—how to look, think, act, and be. You will be shocked.

The shock is necessary if you are to develop the discipline of a disciple. A disciple cannot stay in a private self. A disciple is committed to seeking the God WITHIN. The more the student senses her relationship with the God within, the more discipline she will apply to REVEAL the God within.

As this process unfolds, you will start to resonate with others who are experiencing the same awareness, those who have expanded past the boundaries of a private self. You will begin to form or join small groups or gather two or more together for the purpose of developing a soul family to support the mutual discipleship.

Members of your soul family will be connecting with members of other soul families who truly see themselves as disciples—for there is a common tongue, a common note, if you will, a common place in the heart of the disciple. Disciples recognize each other.

Do not mistake people to be disciples of the Ascension Process because they may have gifts and talents, such as channeling, teaching, and entertaining, but they have not put the yoke on with the discipline and entered the state of a disciple. The state of being of a disciple says, "There is nothing else more important to me than my spiritual tools. There is nothing more important to me than putting my yoke of discipline on today. There is nothing more important to me than entering the state of grace of collective consciousness."

You will see great polarization for a period, which we will loosely call the Ascension Period. You will see many people with great gifts and talents who are NOT putting the disciple inside of themselves first. They are simply not choosing discipleship to be the most important thing. So as you continue, in the vernacular of this channel, to "move and shake" in your soul family, connecting globally with other soul families, discern very carefully who recognize themselves as true disciples in the mission and who are simply PLAYING with their gifts and talents. There is a substantial difference.

The Ascension Process means that the people who choose it have understood themselves to be part of the whole, and that not choosing Ascension is, in human terms, a way of letting God down. It is a way of completely disowning their divinity. Anything less than choosing Ascension is a disservice to the very nature of their being. So, of course, when we speak from the fifth dimension from this particular frequency of the Two Marys, we will be very clear about this distinction, and you will see many not choose who say they are for their Ascension Process.

J: You have defined the Ascension Process in our past conversations, and I have read many definitions elsewhere. Would you define it again so that we may provide a common understanding for everyone?.

M: Simply put in very human terms: Ascension means to move beyond the present state of being, whatever that is, to a higher order of integration such that you become more whole, more complete, and more surrendered to your connection with the divine for the sole purpose of expressing that divinity.

Indeed, Ascension might mean, for many humans, ascending beyond the ego. If the ego is what keeps the human trapped in lack and limitation, and indeed it is true, then Ascension would mean moving beyond the ego into limitless freedom, limitless empowerment, and limitless ecstasy and joy.

That is the intention of these discourses. We give you and all the students our most enthusiastic blessings at this time as you continue on your journey of Ascension.

BREATHE

DISCOURSE TWO

BALANCE YOUR GIVING AND RECEIVING EVERY DAY

J: Though we have talked about this before, I would like to start from the beginning and ask some basic questions to help ground everyone in some common understandings. Who are the Two Marys, what is your mission, and why have you joined energies?

M: The Two Marys are a specific entwined frequency of Ascension. The purpose of this frequency is to create a bridge for third-dimensional beings to move into higher dimensions, including the fifth dimension and even beyond if that is in their divine soul plan. We exist solely for that purpose. Therefore, we have limits in terms of how we will occur, how we will express, and how we will communicate.

We exist through a channel such as our beloved Jessie, in a very precise, carefully constructed vocabulary. The words we use are the healing agents of the consciousness. If listened to more than once, the words will alter how the brain functions for that individual.

For those who pick up their tools and practice the various exercises, such as breath, movement, and sound and who practice reading the words and becoming the words, they will find that everything they need for their Ascension is all here. For this is a frequency for Ascension. There are many frequencies for Ascension. Ours is simply the frequency that expresses the divine feminine as the way.

J: When we talked about the Two Marys before, we talked about you as Mother Mary and Mary Magdalene. So would you discuss the connection of the frequencies to them?

M: Indeed. The frequencies of Mother Mary and of Mary Magdalene serve on this planet as icons, as beloved symbols of divine feminine love, of true sacrifice, of transformation, of miracle consciousness. If you look at their stories when they walked on the planet, their lives were very unusual by any standard. They were not normal, average girls who became everyday wives and mothers. They were spiritual adepts who had extraordinary gifts, talents, and vision and fantastic experiences.

Indeed, the whole story of Jesus being born through an immaculate conception was not the truth of what happened. It was simply the language for those times translated over time, with a little help from the Church, to take one aspect of what is fantastic and remove it from public access. What was fantastic about Mother Mary was her unconditional love of herself and her connection with the divine, with her beloved husband, and with her family. She was a beacon of love. So, of course, Jesus chose her as his mother.

The immaculateness of the conception was the purity of her love, which was extraordinary. And everyone who came in contact with her knew she was extraordinary.

So, indeed, through the purity of that light she had an immaculate conception while deep in the throes of passionate sexual lovemaking with her husband, her beloved Joseph.

Mary Magdalene was the female equivalent of the Jesus. She was his Twin Flame. She was entirely different her whole life. She was different as a child. As children they (Jesus and Mary) were clear they were going to be together. They needed to grow up, to become appropriate ages, and then they were going to become husband and wife. They never questioned this.

Mary Magdalene was equally pure of love and had a developed intellect and consciousness that made it simple, easy, and fun for her to engage with her beloved Jesus. She regularly had discussions and dialogues that, except for certain spiritual adepts that trained Master Jesus when he was traveling away from home, no one was Mary Magdalene's equal in cocreating and conducting conversations to disseminate to the disciples to then teach to the masses. So she was Jesus's beloved muse, but she was not passive. She was quite assertive.

So you have the frequencies of the assertive energy of the Mary Magdalene and the supreme constancy of the Mother Mary coming through today in this discussion. You will notice an assertive energy that is not masculine. It is the feminine wisdom taking the child by the hand and saying, "Let's go this way. Let's go over here. Let's walk on this bridge to get over this river."

We are conducting ourselves through other channels at this time. There will be similar resonances through every channel of extreme compassion and unity consciousness. We manifest ourselves simultaneously and globally through different nations and peoples, for that is the nature of the fifth dimension.

Because of all the distractions available to humanity at this time, we wish to conduct ourselves more in the "how to" of Ascension, as opposed to stories of the Two Marys, which can be useful. We will refer to them from time to time but only to clarify a point or make it more human. There are new books available for people to study how we evolved and ascended.

J: You can see the value of what you just spoke about though, can't you?

M: Indeed. Integration is the key. When one can integrate, one can move forward. On the same note, we will be that assertive energy leaving the mind behind more and more.

J: Now that you have defined who the Two Marys are, would you explain your mission? You have joined energies and have a joint mission. What would you tell us about that?

M: Our mission when we walked on the planet is the same as this mission—to escort humans into the Christ Consciousness for their Ascension.

J: How would you define Christ Consciousness?

M: Ecstatic union with divine love.

J: Why did you join your energies?

M: We have entwined our energies to provide a powerful expression of divine feminine essence. The process that is going on in our entire universe, as it applies to Gaia and humanity, is the giant rebalancing of the masculine and the feminine energies. On this planet there is so much conditioned thought—and you understand that thought manifests into reality—that is so over the top regarding masculinity. It required bringing about additional frequencies to bring a balance (of the masculine and feminine energies) into the third dimension.

If you consider that the Messiah is looked at as a man, if you consider that the Catholic Church is run by men and only men can belong to the priesthood, if you consider the masculine aggression and corruption on your planet, it becomes instantly clear that additional feminine energies are required to effect change. That is simply our mission. That is why we are manifesting simultaneously to many all over the planet. It is time to join the frequencies of the Mother Earth to the Mother Energy. It is time for the Divine Mother to be known, recognized, and belonged to the same way people belong to their notion of the Christ Consciousness.

J: Your definitions of Ascension in the first discourse are very beautiful, but I believe many churches could have made similar statements about the spiritual experiences they offer. To me the definitions don't really explain the uniqueness of Ascension and why it is happening now on Earth. Something far more cosmic is occurring, in my view, that is not being captured by these definitions. Can you understand what I am saying?

M: Indeed. And we shall address that, beloved Joel. You will notice that we deliver information starting with the lowest common denominator and then moving to higher levels of distinction. So, indeed, there is a cosmic, coordinated expansion that is ongoing in the universe, which is difficult to explain in human language.

Sometimes visual art is more effective than words. Imagine it as a giant birth process, not like a human birth with blood and pain, but a giant flower blooming. If you witness that blooming in slow motion, you see first this petal and then that petal and then all of a sudden there it is in all of its glory—all the petals open, its full expression of all its incredible beauty and radiance. That is happening in all galaxies simultaneously.

So, you see, the expansion and Ascension of this planet is connected to the expansion and the Ascension of all planets. There is nothing separate anywhere. There is no little private galaxy over here that is not connected to this giant birth process, this giant collective dance, this giant self-expression. So the game of Ascension for humans is to align their self-expression with this dance, for humans have been self-expressing all over the place forever.

The vast majority of that self-expression is from the small, private self. This is not the self-expression we are speaking of. We are speaking of authentic self-expression, which occurs when one is harnessed to that I AM presence, when one is in alignment with one's divine soul path, when one is a disciple to one's Ascension Process. That full expression becomes the giant birth process, the giant flower that is blooming.

J: If it is engaging the whole universe, why now? What is happening in the entire universe that makes this the time of Ascension?

M: Let us discuss human birth as an analogy for this question. In the human birth process, there is a point after much contracting where the child enters the birth canal. If all is going well, there is a limited time in the birth canal, and then out comes the infant.

So why now is because the time of contracting has completed. It is a time of collective consciousness moving to its next order of integration. It has been that way forever. It will always be that way.

So this time—the end of all the ages, the end of duality, the end of cause and effect being what governs humanity's thoughts, what shackles humanity to lack and limitation, greed and avarice— that time has completed. Now we are in the birth canal. So every planet, every species, everything that exists in reality exists either completely in congruency to universal law or is in contraction. Then there will be the birth canal and then the birth into universal law. It is the way. In simple human terms, God always wins.

There will always be a return to love. But if there is separation from love, there will be contraction. The very nature of separating from love is to contract, is it not? When one ceases to separate from divine love and enters the flow of collective consciousness expanding into higher orders of ecstasy and bliss, there is no desire to contract ever again.

J: Does humankind have any influence over this giant cosmic process?

M: Humankind does and does not. Ultimately, everything is expanding and nothing will stop that ever. That is the nature of the universal source. So can humans throw a monkey wrench into the machinery of that? Absolutely not. Can humans separate in consciousness from the ecstatic union of that? Clearly. Will that ultimately prevent that individual from experiencing divine bliss? No, that soul will continue to go through the contractions, through cause and effect, through laws of Karma, until it chooses to enter the birth canal. It is always a choice.

J: Does that decision have anything to do with those larger cycles of 26,000 years and others we've been told about? We're told that this opportunity for Ascension won't come again for a very long time. Is it up to each person to decide when to go into the birth canal, or are we influenced by these larger cosmic cycles?

M: As you may have detected, there is an influence with larger cycles, and there is an influence with peer groups. So there is a combination of energies moving in that direction, pulled much like things on planet Earth are pulled by gravity. There is a giant opening as this 26,000-year cycle completes. There are expansions within your solar system. There are phenomena that are happening, including with your sun. So yes, indeed, there are natural forces, coupled with the intense duality on this planet, that are creating such a large opportunity. For humans tend not to choose transformation until their suffering is at maximum.

J: I think you have just created a wonderful spiritual context for *The Ascension Handbook*.

M: Indeed. To be of service truly means to be of service with the cosmic dance, not just the dance on this planet. The planet is your gateway, your spaceship, if you will. She is alive, and she is in her expansion. So it is simply about aligning yourself with this large energetic complete ecstatic bliss that has no beginning and has no end. This notion is very foreign to many who will pick up *The Ascension Handbook*.

Most who are attracted to spiritual communities and discussion groups in mystery schools like the one you are involved in are still completely embedded in the notion of THEIR life—this private life of theirs, their mortality, and the angst and drama surrounding that versus something within their heart that recognizes a greater truth. The study of immortality versus mortality is such a taboo on your planet. Do you see?

J: Well, yes. Even The Life Mastery Program* is pretty much focused on how to make the most of our life here. We refer to Archangel Michael, of course, as the source and the ultimate goal of creating a world of community, harmony, and equality. But, basically, the program is designed to help people deal with the issues of their lives.

M: For that is where one must begin. One must begin to take full responsibility for one's life and then develop mastery of love for oneself so that one can become a meaningful contributor to the collective. For it is truly in that contribution to the collective that your essence becomes realized. Is that not true for you, beloved Joel, when you are in the contribution of self with your students? That is when you are resonating with your divine soul plan. That contribution is where the private self has disappeared, has it not?

So as we address this question, how does one stay in contribution to the collective, we acknowledge this is an aspect of self-love. When you love yourself completely, your relationship with yourself is a contribution. In your current times, you speak about it as taking care of yourself, being good to yourself, and positive self-talk. Indeed, these are congruent with contributing to oneself. To fulfill and ascend, one must be in contribution to oneself, one must be in contribution to others, and one must be in contribution to the divine cosmic plan. This is the fulfillment of Ascension. It is in three parts.

* See Link to Angel News Network.

Contribution to self, indeed, is the fundamental teaching of the Life Mastery Program. How to become a master in contributing to self such that the self expands in consciousness beyond that private self and has a desire, indeed a longing, to contribute to others. For it is only in authentic self-love that one can truly give in contribution to others.

This is discussed in everything from Archangel Michael's teachings to every great spiritual writing and sacred teaching. If one is giving to get, one is still stuck in the private self, and one is in lack and limitation and is not in surrender to self-love. When one is surrendered in self-love, the giving and the getting are all the same. There is no distinction. It is all beingness. It is all blissful.

J: Thank you for that wonderful teaching. Are we ready to move onto the next lesson?

M: We wish to discuss again the purpose of discipline, which is, of course, to contribute to one's freedom. To do that, one has to address the human conundrum: "This is the thing I long for the most, yet this is the thing I resist the most."

For us to effectively address discipline, we have to invite the student to investigate her own relationship with freedom/ Ascension, to delve into and explore, "What are my resistances? What are my fears? If Ascension and freedom mean immortality, what nonsense have I sold myself through the cultural mythology regarding mortality, suffering, sacrifice, freedom, and bliss?"

So every student must ferret out what are the ways that he, consciously or not, actively resists the thing that he desires the most. So the discipline is to stay disciplined in the inquiry. If you were baking a loaf of bread—we will use an analogy here—what are the ingredients that would belong in Ascension? The most obvious ones, besides discipline, are self-love and forgiveness:

To forgive oneself for resisting what one longs for with all of one's heart.

To forgive oneself for buying into the collective unconscious, the hypnotic, destructive pull of the cultural norm.

To forgive oneself for worshipping one's mind as the absolute end all, thus cutting oneself off from supreme intelligence in the heart.

To forgive oneself for thinking that the cosmic collective consciousness did not matter.

To forgive oneself for thinking there were not other beings and places, interconnected, all relying on cooperation.

To forgive oneself for thinking one does not deserve love.

To forgive oneself for thinking one's God had a light switch that would be turned on or turned off regarding God's love. "When I'm good, God loves me. When I'm not good, I am not loved."

So to truly love oneself, one needs to be in a constant state of forgiveness. Indeed, our lives on this planet, as the Two Marys, became powerful experiences in forgiveness. Forgiveness was the way of being that got us through—self-love, self-forgiveness. Whenever there was conflict within our group, the only acceptable response was to love and forgive—and forgive as fast as possible.

We led this discourse with discipline because everything that we shall teach from this point forward requires discipline. This discourse is not new information. It is simply being repeated in a way that is simple to understand. If you are suffering, if you are not experiencing the fulfillment you long for, then you must start forgiving yourself for not having what you long for.

So we recommend that whenever you catch yourself not in fulfillment, you instantly say out loud to yourself, "I forgive myself for that." Look in a mirror deep into your eyes and say, "I forgive myself for that." Can you see how this can help you begin to take responsibility for your own reality?

J: Yes, I do. I also see how that can begin to reshape our instincts to forgive others rather than to judge or blame them.

M: Indeed. Forgive yourself for being upset at that other. For it is you who chose to leave paradise for that judgment. Interesting way to think about it, is it not? It is the individual who chooses to leave ecstatic union for the sake of separation and judgment. It is a mature individual who chooses to stop that behavior because it is in defiance of universal law, which is to love yourself completely.

J: This teaching certainly relates to the hardships you endured when you walked with Jesus.

M: Indeed. Many would point, laugh, shout, and throw stones. Yet every bit of that world was sacred. It would not serve our mission to allow ourselves to traffic in the judgment of those individuals throwing those stones, shouting hateful words. It was not congruent to our mission to respond with anything but love and forgiveness.

J: In the light of what you have told us, it's quite shocking how poorly Mary Magdalene has been depicted in scripture and religious teachings, which have distorted our understanding of who she was and what she represented.

M: Indeed. She represents the avatar in human form. She is one of many avatars that have taken human form as female and walked on the surface of our beloved Gaia. She is truly the symbol of the female avatar.

J: What is an avatar?

M: The avatar is a master teacher who has a direct conduit, a direct pipeline, if you will, to supreme intelligence. The avatar is an evolved soul, a multidimensional being, who is here on your planet as a master teacher. And so, of course, the Church, which corrupted many of the teachings of the mission, cast her as a lowly prostitute, for a patriarchal mission cannot have a female who is accepted and known as an avatar.

It would have been impossible to succeed as an exclusive patriarchal cult if they had acknowledged and included someone like that who, for the times, was unacceptable. Everything in that region was influenced by patriarchal religion. Even the Jewish faith as it was taught to Jesus had very strict laws regarding what women could and could not do, touch, and so on.

J: Women were pretty much kept in the kitchen, weren't they?

M: Indeed. And then banished to the red tent at certain times of the lunar cycle. Female avatars are now surfacing on your planet because it is no longer as acceptable to subjugate and dominate them, though there is still a great deal of this. You can see the many empowered and fulfilled women serving as mouthpieces for transformational messages—transforming humanity out of the mess into congruence, community, and cooperation versus competition. And they are multiplying at an enormous rate. In a way, women are using the symbol of Mary Magdalene to rise from the subjugation that is cast upon them into the role of the avatar. Do you see?

J: I see that. I also see the importance of including this information as part of the spiritual context for the balancing of the masculine and the feminine.

M: Indeed. For within the masculine is always some level of subjugation of self, is there not?

J: There is for me.

M: Indeed. So the balance truly occurs when the two are connected as one. When we say the word *balance*, the easy visual is a set of scales. For most their concept of the balancing of the masculine and feminine energies would be a set of scales with one side the feminine and the other the masculine. The balancing is the constant movement back and forth. That is not what we are teaching.

We are teaching the unification of those dual aspects so that every being has the power to shift from one to the other at any point, at any time, being in the expansion itself. It is only with the merging that there is complete congruency with the expansion of the cosmic consciousness. It is not through two things bobbing back and forth. That is not expansion into the collective.

Expansion into the collective occurs when both aspects are joined together and the individual is free to move into the expansion, bringing the feminine ability to embrace the unknown while, at the same time, being the masculine directional—let us move forward and investigate this and experience that. So this visual of the set of scales is not useful. We prefer you to see it more like the six-pointed merkaba where in the midst of all the geometry is this swirling energy. That is the merging of the masculine with the feminine.

J: We have been discussing the need for discipline in the Ascension Process. Have we completed that?

M: We wish again to say that when one experiences oneself as suffering, one is in defiance of universal law; therefore, it is an individual's responsibility to forgive oneself for childishly acting out in defiance of divine love. One must forgive oneself and surrender to divine law. It is that simple. How will one know one has surrendered to divine law? One will not be suffering.

There will be some who are more naturally attuned to this law and this truth. There will be others who require great effort, using discipline to pick up their spiritual tools, which are designed strictly for the purpose of preparing one's consciousness for expansion. So there is always a choice.

If they are not ready to apply discipline to pick up their tools, they will not read further in this manual. That is their choice. This is a manual for those willing and able to pick up their tools. For those who are stamping their feet and throwing temper tantrums, refusing to pick up their tools, there are other places for them to go to exist.

These teachings are for adults who are clear: "I am done with suffering, with being a small, private person disconnected from the whole. I am interested in being part of a giant expansion. I am interested in moving past the brainwashing and finding out who I am as I give myself to divine love, as I give myself to the collective consciousness."

J: That is beautiful. What would you call the next teaching?

M: The next teaching is called BALANCE THE DAY. There are many teachings in your culture about creating balance in your life. However the challenge of actually living a balanced life in your contemporary culture is something of a joke. It is not a joke to the fifth-dimensional beings working diligently with the third dimension.

So balance your day means literally BALANCE YOUR GIVING AND RECEIVING EVERY DAY as a statement of your self-love, as a statement of your self-forgiveness, using discipline to enact that. We are speaking to many healers out there. Do not fool yourselves. It is NOT better to give than to receive. That was never a teaching of Master Jesus. The teachings from the fifth dimension always have been:

LOVE YOURSELF SO FULLY THAT YOUR ONLY LONGING IS TO GIVE BECAUSE YOU LOVE YOURSELF FULLY.

Be in the expression of that love, for to be human is to be communal. It is lawful for a human who loves herself to give of herself freely. However, this notion in your culture that it is OK to be harried, hurried, tense, and empty at the end of the day and to wake up joyless is not being of service.

This is a giant disservice that has been so culturally accepted that it is almost like winning a gold medal in the Olympics as to who can knock themselves out the most overdoing that imbalance. If you study some of the avatars who have been spiritual celebrities in your collective consciousness, many of them are struggling because they have not understood this distinction.

They have health crises, their home life is empty, and they are drifting into their egos. Balance the day means literally every day.

This channel was once confronted with gentle kindness by one of her mentors and avatars many years ago when he inquired, "When do you take your bath?" She replied, "I don't take a bath. I have a small infant and I have a practice. I am very busy, so I take a shower." He looked at her and said, "How do you fulfill your breathing exercises in the shower?"

The balance must be every day, not some days, not Sunday, not when you have time. If you choose Ascension, we implore you to be highly organized with your time. At the beginning and end of each day ask yourself:

"Am I fulfilled?"

"Am I doing activities that fulfill me?"

"Am I giving to myself?"

"Am I contributing to others?"

"Am I contributing to the divine plan of the cosmic expansion?"

This must be the practice of the disciple.

J: Might we suggest some simple, specific behaviors that would help people bring balance into their lives?

M: The teaching is the teaching, beloved Joel. We do wish to invite you and this beloved channel to contribute yourselves in each and every one of these teachings with your own observations and suggestions. For example, to honor oneself as God might appear selfish to many. To reduce a forty-hour workweek to a twenty-five-hour workweek might appear lazy to some. To honor the body as a temple by breathing, taking baths, lying on the ground and absorbing energy, contemplating nature and beauty might appear frivolous. But what are the benefits? How do those activities bring one to a blissful, ecstatic union with divine love? For that is always what we will return to. Do you see?

J: Yes, those are simple, easy things people can do, small ways of creating balance.

M: Indeed. So you see what we just discussed requires self-forgiveness. "I forgive myself for thinking it was selfish to honor my body as a temple."

J: We're inviting people to make choices that may diverge from the cultural norms with which we were raised.

M: Indeed. The cultural norm is not about Ascension; the cultural norm is about DESCENSION! Descension into hell, we might add—how to become completely disconnected from everything that has anything to do with universal law. So, indeed, if one is committed as a disciple, one is renouncing the cultural norm. One is washing oneself of it on a daily basis.

J: That was a little jolting when you said many of our cultural norms are not about Ascension but about descension.

M: Indeed. Your cultural norms reflect what is happening on this planet. Look at the extreme amount of aggression and war on your planet. They are simply reflections of your cultural norms. The Light Workers, the Light Warriors, the avatars, whatever you shall call them, understand this and will not participate in the traffic of the cultural norm.

So, indeed, taking action each day to create that balance becomes a supreme act of discipleship, of self-love, of congruency with the cosmic plan, of love expanding into more love, of bliss expanding into more bliss, of freedom expanding into more freedom of expression. That is the purpose of making each day matter as a sacrifice to the divine, making each day sacred.

It might look ritualistic to some such as this beloved channel's insistence on taking a bath each morning might appear ritualistic or frivolous. But it is the consciousness she brings to that act that matters. It is the consciousness you bring, Joel, to the act of your sacred readings when you begin those each day. It is the consciousness you bring to the spiritual exercise.

When people want change, we know from the fifth dimension how to coach and to mentor them for that to happen. That is the nature of *The Ascension Handbook*, coaching and mentoring so that Ascension is inevitable.

BREATHE

DISCOURSE THREE

CHOOSE A COMPASSIONATE RELATIONSHIP WITH GOD

M: *Compassion* means "complete acceptance with an open heart." So we are teaching you to have complete acceptance of God with an open heart. Doesn't this make sense once you realize that you are God experiencing yourself as you? Therefore, the only way to proceed is with a fully opened, compassionate, loving relationship with God. Anything less than that would be a private self, which, as we discussed in the prior discourse, THE SELF DOES NOT BELONG TO YOU. IT BELONGS TO THE COLLECTIVE.

We are opening a space for you to explore being in complete surrender, being in compassion without any mental understanding. The need for understanding reflects the private self that believes it is not safe to proceed without first understanding. That reflects your experience when you "left the garden" after your childhood, after your innocence, when you were shamed and blamed and decided that the only safe place was in the construct of your mind.

Having a compassionate relationship with God is having a relationship with love, which creates. The private self, the mind, focuses on judgment and fear and the lower vibration frequencies which destroy. So choosing a compassionate relationship with God means CONSTANTLY CHOOSING TO SERVE AS A CONDUIT FOR THE ENERGETIC FREQUENCIES OF THE HIGHEST EXPRESSION OF GOD. Less than that is to choose limitation.

Compassion towards God includes joy and the gratitude to be able to serve and be here. It is like the infant's hand, asking for and needing nothing, simply reaching out in joy, gratitude, and acceptance in complete surrender to universal law—love is, love is.

It takes discipline to keep moving forward into that place where the desire is to remain in that open-hearted, compassionate state so that when fear knocks, you can say, "I see you for what you are. I choose to remain here in the state of exquisite union," which, of course, is called GRACE.

Inherent in this teaching is developing a relationship with grace—finding grace in every moment, even when experiencing fear itself. The cosmic joke is it's all love anyway. Instead, humankind has an unconscious commitment to the rituals of lack and limitation—fears, worries, sufferings; fears, worries, sufferings. What if those rituals of limitation were replaced by rituals that catapulted the individual through the death urges of the unconscious mind into ecstatic union, into GRACE?

How would it be if humanity no longer feared death, and, therefore, there were no death? It is the belief system and the worshiping of these rituals that creates death. In a compassionate relationship with God, the rituals become extremely important.

So we wish to ask humanity, where are you engaging in the ritualistic, addictive dance with lack and limitation through thought? If you are anxious, you are doing it. If you are afraid, you are doing it. It is not about NEVER doing it. IT IS ABOUT SPENDING MORE OF YOUR ENERGY PRACTICING THE RITUALS THAT CREATE ECSTATIC UNION.

So will you begin to design your day, your life around the practices that literally open the kingdom? Will you engage the breath, movement, and sound; chanting, dancing, self-love; the mirror exercise in The Life Mastery Program? All tools work when applied with humility and sincerity. It requires a 100 percent commitment. If you have fears or doubts, do as many avatars on your planet have done. Simply observe the thought and return to the garden: "Yes, there it is again, the ego wishing to seduce me into a complete break from ecstatic union."

YOU ARE ALWAYS WORKING ON ONE THING ONLY, THE COMPLETE COMMITMENT TO BEING IN THE GARDEN, IN THE ECSTATIC UNION WITH GOD.

When you start to experience yourself as working on only one simple thing, everything else falls away. The mind is clear in service of the heart, and miracles manifest. But it is from that ONE THING that that is possible. You are God. Your mission is to experience yourself fully—not as a sort of, a kind of God or Goddess, not like you attend summer camp and then go home.

YOUR MISSION IS TO EXPERIENCE YOURSELF AS A COMPLETE EXPRESSION OF GOD.

Instead, humanity is involved in complete expression with SUFFERING. You're good at it. It takes tenacity, complete commitment to return to it over and over. You have the skills. We are suggesting you use those skills to create from the space of love, beauty, wholeness, harmony, resonance, and the community of the Ascension.

It has always been about CHOOSING. And then the sweetest part occurs. You are swept down the river. It is sheer delight, and there is no part of you that can choose anything else. That is Ascension. There is no need to leave the garden. It is complete. It is whole. So we invite you and all the readers to use the following mantra:

I AM WHOLE. I AM GRACE. I AM WHOLE. I AM GRACE. I AM WHOLE. I AM GRACE.

How do you apply these insights continuously? How can you catch yourself when you enter that mine-filled territory of the private self? How can you build warnings that you are walking into that minefield and quickly reach for the tools with full self-expression? Not full self-expression that springs from the lack and limitation of the PRIVATE SELF that generates rage expressed as an eye for an eye, which was never the teaching. That produces violence and war.

No, we are discussing full self-expression of the same rage in a safe way, in a container of love. Full self-expression contained in love means RETURN TO LOVE WILL BE THE OUTCOME of that full self-expression. In the complete balancing of the masculine and feminine, one can have rage and grace simultaneously. One might call it dignity. However, it can LOOK violent, such as beating the pillows or pounding a mattress with a bat or yelling until there is no sound besides the sound of love.

To really understand this work, it is to know that IT WILL ALWAYS RETURN TO LOVE. Force begets more force. Separation begets more separation. Set this boundary for yourself: DO NOT TRAFFIC UNLESS IT IS CONTAINED IN LOVE. That may even change how you discuss your issues with your friends and loved ones.

For example, you are about to have a conversation, which may appear disconnected, separate, and coming from lack and limitation. Tell your friend, loved one, group, "My intention is to return to love. Will you hold the space of my intention for me because I intend to return to love? I am not there yet. Do I have your commitment to listen to me in a way where you and I both know I am committed to return to love? I will do whatever it takes. I will process myself as fast as possible."

This is a powerful assertion. From this point forward, engaging in it will drastically change your life. This will raise the question, "To what degree do I truly want my life transformed in every instant, in every engagement with every relationship I have?" Can you start to sense the profundity of this?

The term *integration* is most specific to this discussion of union versus separation. To move from separation into union, one must become more whole. One must become more "one with." Integration, simply defined, is to become more "at one with," to assimilate the parts that were separate into the wholeness, into the grace.

The separation of humanity can be defined as lack of integration of humanity, failing to integrate universal law, which is to always endeavor to become more at one with God.

BREATHE

DISCOURSE FOUR

DESIGN YOUR DAY TO BE SPIRITUALLY POWERFUL

M: The discourse today is to deepen the awareness, the awakening, one gained from the conversation of the previous discourse, HAVE A COMPASSIONATE RELATIONSHIP WITH GOD, which, of course, implies compassion with self. Because God is all there is, it implies compassion for others. That, of course, is the state of grace to which humanity can ascend.

This discourse is to take it to the next stage, which is "beingness"—the beingness in every moment of compassion and choice. In every moment Ascension is happening. In every moment species are evolving, multidimensional beings are expanding. Everything is ascending whether humanity thinks so or not. So choose consciously in each moment to allow grace, to allow beauty, to allow spaciousness.

We recommend that every student design what we would call a SURVIVAL KIT for your day. This involves discipline and structure, of course. That is why most spiritual adepts come from long years of living in ashrams and temples so they can be so structured that there is nowhere to go but inward to their God.

We are often entertained by the surprising lack of discipline and structure that even very powerful spiritual beings engage in. It is as if they would have a powerful day without designing it to be that way. So this discourse is about literally taking the time to design a SPIRITUAL SURVIVAL KIT for your day.

How do you begin the day? How do you start your relationship with God when you open your eyes? Once you have designed your day, what structures do you need to have in place in the event that you forget and fall from grace? How will you know that you have fallen? Write these things down. What are the signals? Keep them very short and concise: "heart races, palms sweat, throat gets dry, and breathing gets shallow." Don't analyze them. Simply start to train yourself, "What are the signals I need to be aware of to recognize I am disconnecting, so I can then grab a tool and reconnect to engage in 100 percent of full self-expression?"

We have observed that humanity, although mature in some ways, is very much like a small child needing great structure and guidance. Humans need to be taught how to actually live each day. They have forgotten, and there is so much distraction. So the Light Workers, the Way Showers, must have structure and discipline.

How will you get yourself from "the disconnect" back to full, glorious self-expression of the divine love that you are? How will you create that bridge? What is choice A? What is plan B if choice A isn't working and perhaps even plan C?

When all else fails, what will you do? Can you see how valuable it becomes in a spiritual family, in a soul family, in a spiritual community, in any group when each and every person is practicing conscious living for each day?

So it becomes a joy to have a day, but not a concept of joy. It becomes joy FULL. It is very important that the survival tool kit be clear for every adept student. Plan choices A, B, C: "Here is who I will call, not to tell the story of it, but to remind me that I can do choice A, B, and C. I have the courage. I will get the courage. I will use their courage. I will then get off the telephone and do my yoga, put on my yoke."

This concept of living a conscious day has been discussed recently in popular films such as *THE SECRET*. But it goes back to ancient times when spiritual adepts consciously chose every activity and structure in their day.

We understand the mischief of getting too caught up in semantics and literal translations. The context is always the most important thing for the student. Rather than worrying that you don't fully get it, be with the context: "As I plan my compassionate day with myself as God is it feeling loving, peaceful, and enjoyable? Am I loving myself in this process? Am I like a small child saying, 'Oh goody, I get to have a glorious day?'"

We recommend that you state your mission each day out loud with your right hand on your heart chakra. Thank yourself at the beginning of your day for fulfilling your mission that day. Then we recommend that you humbly bow to yourself in recognition of your greatness that you fulfilled the mission you have just stated. Then practice some spirit breath exercises. (See Helpful Hints.)

So that is your ritual and practice at the beginning of the day. It will take approximately three minutes. Carry your survival tool kit with you throughout the day. There are not going to be many items in the survival tool kit. For some it will be only two or three things. For others, maybe four or five. More than five things, you have not followed the discourses. You need to return to them. In the previous discourse, we stated that the student really is at work on only one thing. So if you have more than five tools in the survival tool kit, the mind is scattered and busy collecting things versus PRACTICING those things.

We recommend a quick series of breathing exercises to return you to cosmic consciousness, a quick affirmation, a quick clearing of one's energy field (see Helpful Hints.) Notice that we continue to repeat the word *quick*. It is time for humanity to stop wallowing in separation and to simply move with the tools available. Move, practice, practice, practice.

"At the end of the day when my head hits the pillow, I get to be fully grateful that I have been an adept student. I have been gleefully reaching for my tools, joyfully attending to my duties, singing songs in my heart, breathing into my glorious physical body, thanking myself for being God desiring all of this. Now I can go to sleep at night." Can you imagine what starts to happen to humanity when all humans start thanking themselves for being God?

We recommend that be the final piece of the structure for your day. Before you take yourself to a different dimensional plane as you go to sleep, THANK YOURSELF FOR BEING GOD AND DESIRING ALL OF THIS.

And so, in Ascension the discipline is to consistently, compassionately, and slowly but surely over time SUSTAIN

FREQUENCIES IN THE PHYSICAL BODY that would be miraculous to an average human of this Western civilized culture. When you can sustain those frequencies, it is completely normal to dematerialize and rematerialize. This is completely within reach for those who practice continually over time to increase the frequencies of what the physical body is able to sustain. The physical body is designed for this, beloved students. Your physical form is designed for IMMORTALITY.

More and more humans will start to recognize how much power they can physically have, for example, by practicing conscious breath work. Again we always wish to make the distinction, never confuse power with force—power being that which is divinely given, that which is of God, that which is of divine intelligence. That is the power and the glory. Force is human made. Force is ego, separation, and duality. Force is not empowerment

Imagine teenagers who would normally be getting their kicks from drugs, video games, or caffeinated beverages, if they discovered they could become ecstatic through breathing. Imagine when your aging population discovers that whether they are ambulatory or not they can have ecstasy in their body in a few minutes. Indeed, creating ecstatic union in the body for most people is going to become the most important thing in their lives. Think about it. What else would they want once they know it's available?

J: They can do it themselves. They don't have to get a degree, spend a lot of money, or consult a priest, minister, or guru.

M: Indeed. That is the blessing of the times you are in. It is the ability to take simple, profound pieces of information and broadcast them quickly and thoroughly. Conscious breath work is an example of just one practice. There are many other practices, but if you examine the lessons of every great spiritual path, the breath is central to the teachings. In your culture today, the breath is fundamentally important because the mind is so in front of the heart. The breath allows one to harness the mind and slow it down very quickly.

J: My Archangel Gabriel book is loaded with the word *breath*, but I started noticing it only when I began to work with Jessie. I have seen that word so many times and never really paid much attention to it.

M: It is the same conversation we had earlier in the discourse. When you start to question your relationship with God and when you start to question your relationship with your breath, you see the power. That is when full engagement can start to occur. But it is only because you are questioning your relationship with it now: "*Hmm*, is there something more for me? *Hmm*, I have seen this before. *Hmm*, this keeps coming up," and so forth.

We refer now to the concept of the hundredth monkey. We delight in that term because we know that many people in your culture understand the concept of the hundredth monkey. So imagine when humanity has a hundred groups of people all saying, "*Hmm*, this thing about breath. It shows up in this book. It showed up in that book. It has shown up before in my life." Then it begins to rapidly escalate. Once humanity escalates its desire to have more ecstatic union, we will have humanity in Ascension. Do you see?

J: I absolutely do because the idea of the tipping point is well recognized in our culture. That book has been on the best-seller list for years.

M: Indeed. The culture is wide-awake about what that means. People simply have not had sufficient conversations about this. It is time. It is not simply the frequencies of the Two Marys. It is simply time. Enough people understand the phenomenon of the tipping point. They get it.

J: This material is so powerful, easy, and accessible.

M: Indeed. That is the gift. That is the intention of this frequency, nothing more, nothing less. Strong, clear communication like the firm hand of a mother guiding the child and then removing the firm hand when enough momentum has been achieved so that the child can run through the field in delight.

So that is the discourse: the notion of relationship with God, the notion of relationship with yourself, the notion of thanking yourself for being God that desired all this, the notion of designing your day in a blueprint that is a resonance of your spiritual DNA, that is a holographic harmonic of your soul blueprint, your signature key, your notes, your song.

BREATHE

DISCOURSE FIVE

MAINTAIN A CONSTANT CONNECTION TO SOURCE

M: Feeling your feelings is fundamental to the Ascension Process. By feeling your feelings, you develop the ability to move in and out of different states of being. When you have developed the ability to feel your feelings, you develop the ability to quickly surrender to them. When you are completely surrendered, feelings move in an instant. They move like a cloud that passes across the sun, and the sun shines brightly again.

Feeling feelings is just the first step. The state of being we are truly aiming for is complete NEUTRALITY, complete "beingness." Neutrality is the exquisite state of grace where all judgment, all separation has been completed. Therefore, it is a state of being present.

The state of neutrality is the state from which, from a human perspective, the Karmic load is completely relieved. For humans to be multidimensional, to be complete in their relationship with separation, they must master both sides of the equation—the positive and negative qualities, the good feelings, the bad feelings.

They must master the expression of those feelings to complete themselves so that the reality is simply "being," as opposed to creating waves of disruptive energies, such as fear and anger. To move into multidimensionality, humans must love more than their physical form and their physical expression, more than their emotional body and embrace a state of being that is beyond joy, beyond self-love, beyond happiness, beyond gratitude, beyond even the most beneficial positive emotion.

Humans move beyond all of these into NEUTRALITY, which is the "still point." At this point humans experience themselves in their full connection with source and experience the full recognition of the agreement, execution, and the fulfillment of their divine soul plan. The state of neutrality can be achieved in both the dream state and in the awakened state through INTENTION. The benefit, of course, is that it enables one to move into one source cocreation space.

The work regarding emotional process is mandatory. How will you know when you have done sufficient work in this arena? You will not resist entering into any feelings whatsoever. You will be so moved by joy that you will burst into tears. You will be so willing to feel your anger you exhaust yourself and feel complete. You will do your process at 100 percent of your intention, and you will have 100 percent of the feeling. When you traffic in full self-expression, you will have zero resistance to any feelings.

So, for instance, if we said, "Have the feeling of rage. You have sixty seconds to have that feeling." To what capacity could you go like an automobile from zero to sixty? To what capacity would you be able to engage fully with rage? Or if the instructions were, "Experience 100 percent of your terror around death, destruction, violence, or of being attacked. Whatever terror you can conjure up, let's have a full minute of glorious self-expression of terror."

Do you see what we are saying? This is not being done. There are no places in the lives of human beings where they can simply say, "*Hmm*, today I shall experience all of my terror. I will carve out six minutes of my time, and I will lie down on the floor or on my bed. I will conjure up all the terror I can so I will experience terror in a way that shows me I can experience it and not vanish, not be banished from the kingdom, so to speak. I can simply be and realize there is nothing to fear about terror. It is simply a ridiculously intense amount of energy in the body."

Staying connected with your source is literally about managing your energy. The energy of the body is managed through consciousness. Managing one's energy is the highest gift that one can give to source. In our previous discourse, we discussed that it is about picking up the tools with 100 percent self-expression—developing the skills to manage one's energy, not out of fear but out of great love, great respect, and great humility because God is being you. You are being God.

Energy management is the "how" to stay connected. It is critical for the student to understand that when you are having your feelings, the feelings are still contained in love. We suggest you observe your feelings and simply say after you observe the feelings, "And that is contained in love." It is much like children practicing the scales on their musical instruments.

There is great resistance on your planet to doing the work of the so-called negative emotions—anger, fear, and terror. Even in much-evolved circles of spiritual community, there is very little emotional discharge work being done. Is that because all of those members are living in bliss? No, it is because people don't want to include their dark side, their negative emotions, as part of their connection. Indeed, every emotion is the gateway to the heart, not just the loving ones.

It is time for human beings to start including their emotional process much as they include diet and exercise as fundamentals for living. How many times a day do you experience anger, frustration, disappointment, betrayal, victimization, dismissal? How much time do you spend processing those emotions? Almost none.

So we recommend a dedication to process that is uncomfortable yet critical. Even for many followers of beloved Archangel Michael, they wait for a crisis and then begrudgingly do emotional process work as opposed to scheduling it like a meal or a haircut. Because we participated in the same behavior when we walked on your planet, we understand the lure of the mind to steer away from the importance of inner process and into the head where all these constructs exist to keep each and everyone trapped and confused.

Imagine if each Ascension student scheduled six minutes a day to discharge emotionally. You can start to see how powerful that might be in an individual's life because when one is fully discharged, when one is fully processed, there is no projection.

When we investigate carefully what tends to put human beings in great chaos and conflict, usually the most common denominator is projection.

So when you are complete with yourself, when you have discharged your distress and have entered that state of ease and grace after a wonderful emotional discharge, then you are free to pursue your divine soul path, your divine purpose, which is distinct from what society says. The freedom that you experience when you release the emotional body will move you into that state of connectivity, that state of belonging to your source. That freedom, no matter how short-lived, holds the seed for all potential freedom. And then that seed creates a longing that, if carefully cultivated, will develop into a forest fire of passion and commitment to fulfill your divine soul plan.

Nothing we will ever discuss or recommend will require a great amount of time. We are simply giving you the basics, which, if applied, will yield tremendous results.

There might be a day when you say, "I have my six minutes scheduled; however, I have no anger left. I have no terror left." Then discharge some of humanity's anger or terror. Be a vehicle for humanity's distress, and discharge that. Be a vehicle for the outcries of the wildlife being obliterated on your planet. Feel humanity's suffering, the ones who aren't in this conversation, those who have no ability to read, no food, no water. Discharge your distress for them.

Until there are enough people having these conversations that suffering will continue and intensify. So doing the work is about, literally, doing the work. This channel, at times, becomes frustrated with humanity. Perhaps you, beloved Joel, have had the same feeling. So much unconsciousness, so much energy wasted, so many refusals to see the light, to be the light, to rejoice, to cooperate.

J: Yes, I get upset with the politics of our time where there is so much conflict between the ideas of separation and unity.

M: Indeed. And that stress that you speak of is your opportunity to engage fully with that beast to really experience 100 percent of that feeling. Go to the feelings that were squashed when you were a child. Those feelings must be engaged. Simply becoming stressed is not sufficient for the Ascension Process. Use your stress as an opportunity to move deeply inside that feeling. That starts to move you forward in consciousness.

J: Can we suggest an exercise for that?

M: Indeed. A visual exercise would be best. Find a picture of human suffering on the Internet or a current event. Look at it. Breathe. Stay with it. Feel the feelings as you say out loud, "I created this. I created this. I created this." Allow the feeling to move through 100 percent of your being. Allow the feelings, allow the tears, allow the anguish, allow the suffering, allow the intensity of the feeling to consume you. Breathe with the feeling. Allow it, and as you engage with that feeling, acknowledge the power of claiming, "As God, I created this."

Within minutes of experiencing yourself in your glorious anguish, you will start to experience something more, something greater, the limitless love that the anger was contained in—the anguish, the suffering, the desperation, the brokenness. You will literally start to sense the presence. Stay with it. The entire process may not take more than about ten minutes. Continue breathing. Then thank yourself for being God who created all this.

When humans begin to consider that they are responsible for separation, they are responsible for all the suffering on the planet—not responsible like guilt or shame but responsible as in causing those things through creation, through power—they, as humans, begin to take on their responsibility. They then can see the power is also there to create more joy, gratitude, love, cooperation, community, and belonging,

It is time for humanity to be responsible. And the highest form of being responsible is being connected to the ONE SOURCE. In a very real way, energy would be better spent in a ten-minute process we have just outlined rather than spending ten minutes watching or reading the news and clucking one's tongue saying, "Tsk-tsk, this is a giant mess. When will they get it?"

The sheer power available to human beings by taking responsibility is beyond comprehension for them. We are simply suggesting that they begin that process with fervor and begin to own their relationship with all of it.

There is a most glorious place in the human heart for what we are discussing. It cannot be intellectualized. It must be experienced. It could be described as having one's heart broken open. But even that is insufficient. A fabulous exercise would be to each day choose a new suffering, a new theme. You can see how enormously valuable that would be, perhaps for twenty-one days to experience one's relationship more fully with what is going on "out there."

When you begin to think and grapple with this idea, all of a sudden you start to glimpse something new or different: "Wow, I am responsible. Through my unconsciousness I caused this." Instead of being depressed, however, how about being GRATEFUL that your level of unconsciousness that caused this situation is sufficient to get your attention now? What if people became grateful instead of depressed? There is so much room inside the mind of the average human being for putting the attention outside of self.

We must be very direct about this:

BEING RESPONSIBLE MEANS ENTERING A STATE OF BEING WHERE IT BECOMES MORE AND MORE CLEAR THAT YOU ARE GOD CREATING ALL OF THIS.

This is a very beneficial process to be engaged in. It changes you from the inside out, and that is what is required. Energy management requires a very large context.

The context can only be I AM GOD CREATING ALL OF THIS. I AM DIVINE LOVE LOVING ALL THIS. UNDERNEATH ALL MY CREATION IS DIVINE LOVE.

That is the only appropriate context for energy management. That is the only appropriate context for Ascension.

We, as the Two Marys, want our message to be intelligible and operational—operational because humans who traffic in time and calendars do not have much of that left. There just isn't much time left. God is greatly expanding divine love on every level.

So that sufficient numbers of human beings join in this frequency, it is necessary to have activities and exercises that help the students move quickly into the appropriate context, the appropriate way of being, even the appropriate way to think about themselves:

WE ARE RESPONSIBLE. WE HAVE CREATED. WE ARE CREATING.

The work is completely timely for humanity. All you need to do now is practice, practice, practice.

BREATHE

DISCOURSE SIX

CLAIM YOUR ASCENSION NOW

M: Be aware that your mind will tell you anything about what Ascension actually is. Your mind has already decided Ascension is something not here, not now. Has it not? Your mind has already decided Ascension must be some sort of destination, some sort of place to GET TO.

It is as if the mind becomes an instant should-could-would machine hammering ideas and notions about things being certain ways. It has a potent lock on what reality is. So if your mind has decided that Ascension is someplace to get to, that means that you have NOT decided to CLAIM YOUR ASCENSION NOW.

Ascension should happen after what? Why after? Why not now? The student must be willing to ask, "Why do I think that? Is that infinitely true or just true in my ego? How is it true? Am I resonating with joy, bliss, grace, gratitude, ecstasy, or something else?"

By claiming your Ascension now, you are choosing to harvest your BLISS now, and you are choosing thoughts that are aligned with becoming more, with integrating more, with surrendering more.

Harvesting your bliss is an exercise that, if you choose, can authentically change every relationship from the inside out. Imagine what would happen in groups, workplaces, families, schools, communities, and governments when no matter what the other person is experiencing, the context in which the entire engagement occurs is "I am supporting you in harvesting your bliss now, and I am harvesting my bliss now."

We have mentioned in previous discourses that these teachings about Ascension will always resonate with all other teachings from the fifth dimension. A particular teaching resonates here from beloved Archangel Michael, which is that the individual is either having what she wants or is SUPPRESSING an emotion.

By harvesting your bliss now, you are EXPERIENCING an emotion (bliss) that will, indeed, manifest what you desire—your Ascension now.

The notion that humans have ALREADY ascended is one we propose at this time. Beloved students, in your imagination is it not true that in other time lines humanity has completely ascended? Indeed, it is true.

J: That is very hard for most of us to wrap our minds around.

M: Beloved Joel and beloved students, it is not possible to wrap your minds around that statement. We invite you to not even try.

We invite you, instead, to celebrate, even if it were only a game, that within yourselves you EXPERIENCE the joy and the peace of celebrating the idea that humanity has already ascended. On some level, somewhere, it has already happened. In the imagination it has already occurred.

A KEY PRINCIPLE OF MANIFESTATION IS TO CELEBRATE THAT WHAT YOU DESIRE HAS ALREADY OCCURRED.

Again we invite you: claim your Ascension now. Indeed, you have free will. You can back yourself away and say, "Until my mental mind can wrap itself around this, I cannot participate in this." We say, indeed you can participate. Simply enter the vibration state. It is as simple as if the frequencies were a piece of clothing that you put on. We are saying discard the notion of some enormous mental complexity and enter the frequency NOW.

J: So you're telling us to accept that our Ascension has already happened.

M: Indeed. That is what we are inviting you to do. Celebrate Ascension now. It is not somewhere else. It is NOW. Beloveds, the more you celebrate Ascension now, the more awakenings occur, the more that the constructs that were limiting and restraining fall away, the more the shackles from earlier egoistic states fall away. So the invitation is CELEBRATE YOUR ASCENSION NOW.

See how many moments of bliss you can sponsor for humanity, for the cosmos. "I am a human being having an experience, and I am choosing to harvest my bliss now. I am choosing to not know certain things about all of this. I am choosing to question what I even think I might know so that I can be more neutral, more present and harvest more bliss." Remember, when human beings are harvesting their bliss, they are granting cosmic permission to expand and move into higher orders of integration.

It is time for humans to stop minimizing their contribution to the cosmos. They have been taught and shamed that they are such tiny participants in the cosmic dance. That is not accurate. There is no hierarchy per se. It is time for humans to feel EXCITED about the level of contribution they are invited to have. Remember that your work as a human is the work of the cosmos. They are the same.

It is time for humanity, it is time for you as an ascending human being, to start appreciating the extent to which you participate in the divine plan. We invite you to celebrate your Ascension and appreciate your participation. Have a sense of humor about your daily follies. There will be follies and there will be falls from grace, so to speak. Create intimacy and humor with yourself. Protect both the humor and the sacred, quiet place beyond your mind.

There is a magnificent place beyond the mind where humor actually is created. That is one reason we suggest using a great deal of humor. It is a doorway into the mind from beyond the mind.

If you do not feel or have humor, take advantage of how much creativity is going on in your third dimension and expose yourself to it through your Internet or your friends and relations. It is most important to engage with great humor.

The ability to laugh creates the flexibility to move beyond the mind. There is often unconscious resistance to receiving new information or new truth, which can be neutralized or eliminated through humor. So, students, you will often hold unconscious resistance that you may not realize is there. It is as if we are conditioning an athlete for a great Olympic event, and we must condition all the different aspects of your being. Humor is part of the daily workout along with breath, movement, and sound.

Again, to stay integrated, practice using humor, practice harvesting your bliss now, and claim your Ascension now. The more you choose your ecstasy, the more you choose to harvest your bliss now, the more you surrender, the more all cosmic consciousness expands.

BREATHE

LONG FOR GOD WITH ALL YOUR HEART

J: I see the value of celebrating Ascension now. However, I was a little confused when you said in the last discourse that we think of Ascension as something we are going to arrive at in the future as opposed to something occurring now. All the spiritual teachings I have read speak about Ascension as a goal we are aspiring to, not a state that exists now.

For example, in *The Seven Sacred Flames* by Aurelia Louise Jones, Adama estimates that there might be a few million people out of nearly seven billion people on the planet who would ascend by the year 2012. He says, "None of you will be lifted into the Ascension Process until you have met all of the requirements and have reached this frequency in your consciousness no matter how long it takes in the cycles of time." So the teachings I have seen refer to Ascension as something we are aspiring to, not something we have already achieved. That is why I am confused.

M: Indeed. It is a common conundrum. Let us discuss what it truly means to be at choice in the now. That is the crux of the distinction we made. To be at choice in the now literally means that one has achieved certain states of consciousness. It is not to say that Ascension is happening now if one is in one's ego practicing duality. Then one is not in Ascension now. One is actively choosing DUALITY. That is one's choice, but that is NOT the proper consciousness to experience Ascension in the NOW.

Experiencing your Ascension now requires using the tools that will get you to the place where you choose to REMOVE duality from your consciousness. It is about practicing rituals and tools that EXPAND YOUR CONSCIOUSNESS AND INCREASE YOUR FREQUENCY—such as breath, movement, and sound, along with meditations such as the glorious meditations in *The Seven Sacred Flames*. These are practices or rituals that create the environment of that now still point, that place where all possibility lies.

Beloved Joel, beloved students, it is most challenging for humans who have not ascended to understand the concept of still point where all possibility and all probability is. You are a most intelligent human being, beloved Joel. Can you see how completely unknown that place is for you?

J: Yes, I have only a vague idea of what that is.

M: Indeed. It comes only through diligent practice. That place of being in the now is fleeting for even very adept spiritual students. A large part of what the Two Marys' conversation for humanity is about is yes, we know the experience of the still point is fleeting at this time for you. If and when you choose with utter passion, utter longing in your heart to increase and to continue to expand your container beyond the mind, beyond the ego and connect with the light body, then it will be understood. Then it becomes a simple, "Oh yes, we understand what this is. Let's keep going."

Until then it is as if the now moment is something like a destination you are striving towards. Is the now moment available now? Indeed it is but only when the student moves beyond the mind and utilizes her energy body as opposed to just her physical body in the third dimension. And we must stress that the physical body in the third dimension is a portal that one utilizes to enter the light body.

So Ascension is happening now. It is available now. It is your destiny now. The invitation is will you JOIN now? Ascension is in the present moment. It is in that still point, and simply practicing increasing your ability to be in the now moment is all that is required.

So we ask, how often do you experience yourself FREE in that now moment? Is it once a day, once a week? Is it occasionally, but you can't remember the last time? When is it? For the discourse today is exactly the next step to this conversation. Is there more inquiry on the topic?

J: Thank you. I wanted to ask about something else you said last time that I don't understand. You said, "In your imagination is it not actually true that in other time lines humanity has completely ascended? Indeed, it is true." Can you clarify that statement?

M: That is a fabulous question, beloved Joel. We delivered that information for the purpose of creating peace of mind for the student. If it has already happened, how would you feel? How would you behave? If you knew it had already happened, you would feel a sense of confidence, of trust, of security, a quieting of the mind and the experience of joy and gratitude for the space.

The discourse for today is fully feel and express deep in your heart the KNOWLEDGE that Ascension has already happened. Fully feel, "Wow, it has already happened. I am already ascending." Feel the gratitude and joy of knowing, "I already have choice. I already have freedom."

Now, we will deliver very important information here. Students must be willing to experience the LONGING in their hearts for that freedom, for that joy. For the students to truly feel the joy and gratitude that Ascension is happening now, they must embrace at the deepest primal level of their humanness the longing in their heart to return home, to be in that state of self-realization, to be in full communion with their I AM presence. The longing must be fervent. It must be potent. It must bring you to your knees. The longing, beloveds, is the fuel. The longing is the road home.

It is time for human beings to experience their longing with all their hearts. The longing in humanity has been misplaced for quite some time. Longing has been misdirected into political longing, socioeconomic longing, longing to conquer a territory, longing to obliterate a population, longing for all kinds of third-dimensional outcomes. And all of this is going on while the soul is longing for the owner/occupant of the body to wake up and say, "Oh, I understand now. My longing for God is everything. My longing for God is all that matters."

Beloved students, God longs for you to be at peace and to experience Godness. When you experience your longing in a pure, unsuppressed way, the door opens and you are immediately expanded into a new state of being that is at once familiar because it is the doorway home. At the same time, there is a new sense of gratitude and ecstasy.

In your everyday lives, there are fabulous ways to cultivate the recognition of the longing. Fervent prayer is perhaps the best means for humanity. We mean by that the student is not simply reciting the words. The words, of course, open portals and create multidimensional process. However, there is more that can be utilized.

Part of today's discourse is to invite students to truly utilize being EMOTIONAL with your prayers. Not emotional as in the ego dictating victimhood: "Oh please, dear Lord, deliver me from this horrible situation that I am in." We are speaking of the pure heart emotional awareness, such as "Oh Lord, God of my being, without you I am nothing. Without you I have nothing. Without you I am trapped in illusion with no possibility of fulfillment ever. So, dear Lord God of my being, I surrender to you with all of my intention, with all of my discipline, with all of my heart's desire."

There have been many teachings in ancient as well as modern times of the secrets of the power of prayer. The fundamental notion of the power of prayer is:

THE OUTCOME HAS ALREADY OCCURRED. WHEN THE DEVOTEE ASSUMES THE OUTCOME OF THE PRAYERS AND EXPERIENCES THOSE FREQUENCIES IN THEIR PHYSICAL BODY, THAT ASSUMPTION AND THAT PHYSICAL EXPERIENCE OPEN PORTALS FOR THE MANIFESTATION OF THE OUTCOME.

The Two Marys invite you, the student, to be in your emotional body in your prayers. FEEL your heart's desires—whether it is a prayer from a sacred book, whether it is your own individual prayer, whether you are praying to your I AM presence, whether you are praying to your source, whether you are praying to Gaia. Whatever your prayer is directed towards, take into your physical body the GRATITUDE of the outcome, the gratitude of truth, such as "I know I belong to God. My truth is I am God."

This is the most challenging aspect of spiritual advancement:

TO TRULY PHYSICALLY FEEL THE EMOTIONS OF KNOWING YOU ARE GOD.

Beloveds, when you start to experience even a small fraction of that truth, the ecstasy is unbelievable. So the Two Marys are counseling students that continuously applying the same tools over and over, year after year will produce greater and greater consciousness. It is as if someone has handed you the keys to the vault. These are universal teachings. And when you realize you have been handed the keys to the vault, is there not great gratitude and joy? Indeed there is.

Our invitation is START PRACTICING WITH GREAT INTENSITY JOY, GRATITUDE AND THE KNOWLEDGE THAT YOU ARE GOD. The more you practice this, the more you will actually experience the different dimensions. You will start to see with your Third Eye these different temporalities, these different time wavelengths and see humanity in them. Of course, God always brings you home. There is no separation. You are already home.

Indeed, that will become clearer as you practice. If you choose to follow this direction, you are going to be more emotional. Not stamping your feet like a small child and whining, "When is our government going to blah, blah, blah? When is the world going to wake up and get it?" Not that. That is ego. That is the lure of the illusion.

We are pointing to something completely different. We are saying be in the HEART. Let the heart lead. Feel your heart opening. Feel the tears as your heart truly opens. Feel the tightness in your chest as your heart opens. Feel and use your breath to keep your heart opening. Do not be afraid of the tears. They are tears of recognition. They are tears of knowing that you have always belonged, that you have always been God.

You will be weepy at times and unwilling to engage in conversations or activities outside of your spiritual truth or what you know your path to be. The weeping will be about gain, not about loss. The weeping will be about such relief that truth is finally showing up in your soul journey in a way that is real and palpable and in a way that will allow you to be complete in this lifetime. You can then move off the Wheel of Karma, which is the law of duality.

The expansion through the emotional body into the heart is mandatory for Ascension. Breath work, sound, chanting (particularly in Sanskrit), certain musical instruments, such as Tibetan bells and chakra bowls, are all helpful. Moving the body, stretching, breathing, and yoga postures are helpful as well. Moving through the emotional body deep into the heart is mandatory. Your truth is revealed, and you will know ecstasy.

One caution: Part of the ego wishes to disturb this process and wishes to say, "Enough feeling the heart. Enough tears." Be aware the ego will attempt to thwart your destiny. Do not trust those thoughts. They are products of the ego and the mental body.

Use your emotional responses to those thoughts as a portal into your heart. For example, if you're thinking a limiting thought about your spiritual progress such as, "I do not have time today to breathe," or "I do not want to meditate today," stop to experience fully the feelings that go with those thoughts. Use your breath to disengage the mind and allow your body to integrate those feelings and thoughts. The breath will make that process easier. As you practice it becomes easier and easier.

You will feel resistance. The ego's resistance is to remind you who you really are. Use your feelings to bring you back into your heart, back into your gratitude. When you have completed the breath work, you will feel the gratitude in your body and in your heart. You will experience it as bliss or ecstasy. This process may take three minutes or thirty. The more you practice, the quicker it goes, the faster you can drop the ego and return to your heart space and move with that longing into your true self.

Students, there will be many things happening over the next several months and years. Do not deny your feelings. Amplify them through the breath. Your feelings are the portal. Underneath all anger, fear, terror, hatred and disregard is divine love. Our invitation is to jump in. Do not stick your foot in and pull it back and say, "It's too scary or stressful."

Indeed, the alternative to using your feelings and working with your breath will be agony. As we have said, the time is up for those seeking fulfillment to hold back. Students who decide not to utilize their breath and not to see and follow their feelings as a gateway to their heart will experience much suffering.

We are not here to stop suffering. We are here to allow those who have the eyes to see and the ears to hear to understand that their longing to be at one with their source is the most important thing. We are here to expedite and assist that process. We are here to provide you with a timeless, infinite process so that no matter what you are experiencing or feeling, you can open this book to any page, read just a paragraph, close the book, feel your feelings, use your breath, and experience yourself transmuting into a higher order of integration, into ecstasy, and into your heart space.

We understand that while all are chosen, only a small fraction will continue to choose. That is perfectly acceptable. As we said, we love to remind humanity of the hundredth monkey. It is absolutely true that when a certain amount—and it is a small fraction—of the population "gets it," a phenomenon occurs and everyone gets it.

This has been proven in quantum science and written about widely. It is called anthropomorphic resonance. So, students, be a member of that small causal fraction stepping up and saying, "Yes, I understand. I don't need my mother, father, sister, brother, or lover to get it. I need to be only one tiny fraction of a small portion of the population to get it, and all humanity gets the gift."

Think about it. In the time of our beloved Jesus, only a small fraction of the population got it, and look how today people are still getting it. Consider the Buddha and his ability to speak and build a following. The entire world was not connected to the Internet listening to the Buddha, with everyone getting it simultaneously. Yet, today, people who practice the universal truth the Buddha spoke of are getting it.

Therefore, we implore you, students, to relax about what everyone else is doing. Be the odd man or woman out. As you say, you'd better believe it you are the odd man out, and that is fabulous. Through anthropomorphic resonance you, your dolphin friends, and many, many other invisible entities are all assisting and creating that field, and all humanity gets it. And yes, beloveds, it can happen in an instant.

We wish to acknowledge that since you, the student, have arrived at this particular place in this particular discourse, it is time for you to be truly recognized.

You have been choosing. You have been chosen. Let go of any notion of how this SHOULD be. Recognize that a small portion of the entire population creates the shift and then everything shifts.

We recommend you start to confront the truth that the Gaia has already shifted on the energetic dimension and that these transformational occurrences are now manifesting in the physical third dimension for the Gaia. Students have the ability to utilize their connection with the Gaia through their imagination and to anchor themselves in that reality that the Gaia has already shifted. If the Gaia has already shifted, if your home on your spaceship Earth has already shifted on the energetic level, can you accept the notion that YOU ALSO have already shifted on the energetic level? It's simply a process of integrating that into the third dimension, much as your Gaia is integrating on the third dimension.

There will be more changes for the Gaia, and she has every capability of integrating these changes. Use that as your mirror, beloved students. Accept that you have already done the work on the etheric level. If you are here in this conversation, it is true that you have shifted. It is time to integrate the shift into the third dimension and let the third dimension be the portal to take you forward with the shift.

The grace of the fifth dimension is infinite. We invite you to breathe that grace into your body. Allow that grace to nourish you constantly. You do not need to wrap your mind around that. Let your body remember it. Your spiritual DNA remembers grace. Your heart knows it as a simple truth. Utilize grace as the giant mystery that your mind cannot wrap around but delivers you home.

Indeed, count on the miracle of grace. If you are practicing, there will be grace. If you are following belonging in your heart, grace shows up.

YOU DO NOT HAVE TO UNDERSTAND UNIVERSAL LAW FOR UNIVERSAL LAW TO WORK.

That would be a great bumper sticker for your automobiles. Just because you don't understand universal law doesn't mean it's not working. It is working. It is working in your life. It is working with humanity. It is working on your planet. Universal law works. So, beloveds, grace moves you. You practice. Grace arrives. Start to enjoy the grace that is showing up. Let your heart move your emotional body.

It is almost as if the heart must massage the emotional body through all its kinks and sore places and boo-boos. Allow it. Allow the tears. Allow the heart to feel as if it is breaking. It will not break. It is simply breaking the constraints that you have placed upon it for millennia. Allow it to hurt. Allow the hurt to remind you you're going home.

Our greatest joy, beloveds, is to assist you in returning to your true spiritual home, your true I AM presence. For the student who reaches this point, know that the entire fifth dimension is rejoicing.

Know that we, indeed, are inspired by your courage. Know that we are with you. We are your best cheerleaders.

Know that we still acknowledge that most of humanity does not utilize the fifth dimension to its full extent and capability. That will come in time for some and then for all with practice.

Emotionalizing your outcomes becomes normal, easy, becomes, as you say, no big deal. Yet it is mandatory. Emotionalize your prayers. Be fervent. Put 100 percent of yourself into your invocations. Invoke with everything you have, and then invoke some more. The blessings are bountiful. You will be delivered.

J: You clarified how to maintain a connection with source so beautifully.

M: This particular teaching is not unique; however, it is timely. Humanity is so distracted with the day-to-day pulling apart of the third dimension, and that is understandable. We have been human, and we understand the lure of those distractions. However, the more one emotionalizes outcomes, the less those distractions distract.

Imagine what happens to anthropomorphic resonances when enough people fervently pray to see their government as whole and capable. Imagine what happens. We have witnessed through your amazing YouTube on your fabulous Internet instances where simply through chanting to the patient, "You are whole, you are whole," tumors disappear in only minutes. How? By acknowledging that simple truth and leaving behind the dualistic notion that the patient was NOT whole.

Since you are God, beloveds, does it not make sense that you can perform any so-called miracle? Of course, for the fifth dimension these are not miracles at all. This is simply trafficking in universal law and universal truths. For humanity they are called miracles, as indeed they were when we walked on planet Earth. Miracles are simply what are true.

So, students, begin to practice simply. Start with small baby steps. Perhaps you have a physical ailment. Start reciting, "I am whole, I am whole" when that ailment occurs. Perhaps you have an injury that hurts in your back. When the back hurts start saying, "I am whole, I am whole." Being whole is being here in the now. It is the same thing.

There are those on your planet who understand this so-called secret who practice and teach it. That, of course, is what we did in the time of Jesus with his so-called laying on of hands. He was simply inviting them, invoking them into the reality that they were whole. Some of the words have not been bastardized in your bible. If you read the words he spoke, you can surely see that is what he was saying, doing, and being:

THE PLANET IS WHOLE. HUMANITY IS WHOLE. YOU ARE WHOLE.

BREATHE

DISCOURSE EIGHT

UNDERSTAND NOTHING AND GAIN EVERYTHING

J: In past discourses you have discussed the hundredth monkey theory (anthropomorphic resonance) and its effects on consciousness and the Ascension Process. Where does this phenomenon come from?

M: It comes from consciousness. It springs from the unified field that connects everything. Of course, what is that unified field? It is God. So anthropomorphic resonance is simply one of the universal laws of God, which is everything is connected. Therefore, all frequencies connect. That is why someone can be meditating in Egypt and energetically connect with someone in South Carolina. It is the unified field through which that occurs. Anthropomorphic resonance is not unique to planet Earth. What is unique to planet Earth is the number of living entities that hold the field and engage from that field with consciousness and knowledge.

When you watch a flock of birds moving in one direction and in an instant they all make a sharp turn and fly in a completely different direction, that is anthropomorphic resonance. In the same way a dolphin can come across a boat of stranded boaters and assist. That is anthropomorphic resonance. It is through consciousness or through the unified field.

J: So you're saying there is a huge collective consciousness that contributes to the phenomenon that includes more species than just human beings. Is it all consciousness of all entities on earth?

M: It is indeed. And that is why we must arrive at this discourse, which is UNDERSTAND NOTHING AND GAIN EVERYTHING. How can you possibly understand collective consciousness? We can give examples of it. We can create stories of it. We can recommend that if students are not familiar with the hundredth monkey that they read that material. But that is simply a drop in the bucket, so to speak, of how collective consciousness really works. There are pioneers in this field, as we speak, who are doing great work in this arena.

The message of this discourse is simple. To try to understand it as a human is a trap. Are we saying don't read about it? No, we are saying read about it. Let it spark a resonance in your heart when you read about it. When you review this discourse again, let your mind go. Simply read the words, preferably out loud, and let your resonance move with it. It will come from the resonance in your heart, not a thought in your mind.

So we recommend you let go of the need to understand. We understand what we are recommending is radical. But let go more and more of the need to understand for the purpose of gaining everything in the heart. We have discussed this in each discourse, if you notice, and each discourse builds on all the earlier discourses.

We used the word *discipline* very intentionally. For when you contemplate love, beloved students, is there really anything to understand? There is nothing you can possibly understand in that space of love. As a mother gazes into her newborn's eyes, what does her mind understand? Nothing. Her mind is still while her heart expands and she knows love. Your mind is still as your heart expands and you know love. And love is everything. Therefore, to gain everything you must become disciplined in rejecting the need to understand, and, instead, reach for the heart process.

We are going to ask you to trust that if you need to know something in your heart, it will be there. This busyness of the mind, this complete addiction to sorting it all out for the purpose of judging and determining what is safe is the fastest way to stop consciousness from expanding. It actually stops the expansion. It is much like pressing the pause button on your CD and DVD players. Everything stops and there is an energetic shift. The body's energy field contracts. The endocrine system changes and moves into a fight-or-flight response: "This I approve. This I disapprove. This I choose. This I reject. This makes sense. This does not make sense. Who says that? Why did they say that?" And on and on and on.

You will experience this. We are simply saying remember the pause button. You pressed it. Now depress it again and return to your heart at which point everything you need to understand will be realized. Maybe not in an instant, but as you stay in your heart, you will see, sense, and know what it is you are supposed to understand.

If it resonates, stay with it. If it doesn't resonate, go deeper. Go until you find your resonance, that place where you say, "Ah, now I know. It all makes sense. Now I see why six months ago I was doing that and didn't have a clue that it would lead to this outcome over here. Now I get it."

We have suggested practicing using breath, sound, movement, and simple stretching of the limbs and opening up to more. The purpose is to open the heart to allow the owner/occupant of the body to move into that state where what is known as truth has nothing to do with the mind. You all have experienced giant *ah-has* after you have battled in your mind thinking this is right, wrong, good, bad, and then you finally let go and entered your heart. Then the insight came.

So where are the authentic insights? They are not in the mind. The mind can recapture them. You will remember those *ah-has*, and you can call on them at any time to say, "Now that my mind can remember what my heart knows, let me use the power of my mind to recreate that energy field." That is the purpose of the mind—to recreate the frequencies of that insight. For example, we talked in the last discourse about truly feeling the longing for God in your heart, feeling it as an intense truth that nothing else compares to. When the student has that experience and then asks the mind to remember that experience, the mind has the ability to recreate it instantly. That is one of the greatest purposes of the mind.

THE MIND CAN CREATE WHAT THE HEART KNOWS. That is very powerful. When the heart knows the ecstasy of its connection with God, the mind can create from that. You all have experienced moments of inspiration when you have been doing something and your mind created something based upon that energy field. That is where we recommend you use your mind more and more. The ultimate balancing for humanity occurs when the heart leads and the mind is its servant. And you, of course, beloved Joel, recollect this teaching.

J: Yes, it's a lesson in The Life Mastery Program, Think With Your Heart.

M: Indeed. Now we are illuminating that to another level so you can engage with it more. What does that really mean? How does the mind let go? And how does the heart think?

In actuality the heart does not truly think. The heart simply is the resonant radar, if you will. In your world you have radio towers sending and receiving energy. The heart is much like that. The heart is a receptive space of the Godhead. There is no thought in there. There is recognition of TRUTH in there.

THE MIND IS THE DIVINE INSTRUMENT THAT MANIFESTS THE TRUTHS IN THE HEART. THAT IS HOW ONE THINKS WITH THE HEART. THAT IS HOW THE MIND MOVES INTO SERVICE OF THE HEART.

Artists and musicians have this gift. That is what is occurring in their moments of inspiration and creation. They are thinking with their hearts. Humanity has always elevated those who seem to have the natural ability to think with their hearts. However, most people exclude themselves from that group and either put creative people on a pedestal or judge them saying, "I don't like that song, that music, that portrait" instead of wondering, "Wow! How is it to think with the heart and just create? How fabulous." It is time for more of humanity to say, "This is my path also. I am a true artist painting a canvas of my Ascension Process. Therefore, I choose to engage in this creative process called surrendering to the heart and allowing the heart to lead the mind."

HUMANS WERE DESIGNED TO HAVE TRUTH IN THEIR HEART AND TO CREATE THAT TRUTH WITH THEIR MIND.

Many of the greatest human accomplishments were created by harnessing the truth in the heart and then asking the mind to create from that truth. All of your avatars, your greatest artists, your greatest teachers have completely lost their minds, so to speak. They use their minds to create the truth that resonates in their hearts.

What if you decided to place parts of your mind off limits as an experiment to see what happens when you traffic less and less in those parts of the mind that are not cocreating with the heart and are simply running with the ego, engaging in fight-or-flight responses?

What if you decided enough is enough and you no longer wished to dissipate your energy and decided to put those areas off limits? "I will develop an acute sense of when I have trespassed." We use that word because it is a trespassing. It is a violation of who you really are to wander into those areas without picking up a tool and processing yourself into your heart.

We are not suggesting you will not trespass. We are simply putting it in a new light. When you trespass, pick up a tool to move that trespass experience into the heart. The discipline will build on itself. At first it will look like a Herculean endeavor. Remember, we were human. We understand that.

Start where you are. Decide to place off limits those areas of your mind (some of which you are not in touch with) that are not in service to your heart. Choose not to trespass there. Further, decide that if you find yourself there, you will do whatever it takes to bring those feelings into your heart. You will be back in your heart, and you will no longer be trespassing into the areas of the mind that are designed for duality and separation.

It is awkward at first for we are literally telling you to move through life without your dominant hand. It is now going to be removed. Continue forward with your life. There is a large part of what you think your mind is good for which does not serve your commitment to Ascension. It is contraindicated, so to speak.

So, again, start where you are and simply decide you will, as in the title of this discourse, UNDERSTAND NOTHING AND GAIN EVERYTHING. You can understand nothing about your mind and simply invoke the truth. "I now invoke the truth that I will participate in my mind when it is in service to my heart. I invoke the truth that I have what it takes to practice that discipline. I invoke the power of God within me to exercise that discipline with all the longing in my heart. I invoke that strength. I invoke that elegance. I invoke that ease for myself and that grace will show up. So be it."

From there you need understand nothing, and you will gain everything. You will find yourself more and more refraining from speaking judgments about anything to anybody. You will find yourself saying things like, "Oh, I see how you feel. That's fascinating." Allow that to suffice, as opposed to discussing with great passion: "Yes, but I feel this way and you feel that way." And now we have conflict. How absurd.

It is not about avoiding conflict or deciding judgment is wrong. It is about understanding that is not where you belong. You belong to God. God is counting on you to belong to God. We cannot stress this enough. The entire cosmos is counting on you to belong to God. Your only purpose is to belong to God. Therefore, if you choose Ascension for yourself, you must diligently practice belonging to your heart, belonging to that limitless portal into the Godhead.

The more you practice surrendering; using breath, movement, and sound; and receiving healing work from others, the more you will understand in the heart there is no need to think or know anything other than "I AM GOD." Out of that still point, whatever is in your DIVINE SPIRITUAL BLUEPRINT will nudge itself forward. It will be like a small, beautiful child knocking on your door, "Hello, here I am. It's time for you to create with me. Hello, you feel this. Let us create from there."

So it can be very elegant once one lets go of using the mind improperly. Simply be diligent and disciplined about it. Humanity's mission with the mind is nearly complete. How beautiful is that? For millennia humanity has explored duality and all of the addictions and the iterations of the mind when it is not in service to the heart. DUALITY HAS BEEN SUFFICIENTLY EXPLORED!

You will see more and more human beings looking for ways of bringing themselves into their heart space. You will see more films, books, teachings, practices, and groups starting to recognize that the way your civilization has trafficked in the mind does not work, and judging doesn't work either. Therefore, practicing discipline and marking the territory off limits is the only way you will progress, the only way you will be fulfilled in your life journey.

The heart will take care of the details. We cannot stress this enough. The heart will take care of what each of you is called forth to manifest. The heart knows. You must spend time there. You must be willing to just hang out there and to do whatever it takes to be there and to mark your territory clearly with intent and to love yourself when you trespass—not just love yourself as an apology for trespassing, but love yourself with your tools that return you home to your heart.

When you see yourself as the master creator, when you see yourself as the obvious candidate for the heart and the obvious candidate for Ascension, the discipline becomes far easier.

Now we will tell you this: beloved students, YOU are the obvious candidates. Know that and mark any other territory off limits. You are the ones who are choosing to move yourselves with great speed. Mark any other territory as unacceptable. The more you stay conscious that you have chosen and that all of God, all of the cosmos, all of the different dimensional entities support this and give grace to this, then the trespassing becomes less and less and eventually you become bound to the Godhead in your heart. That is, of course, the culmination of the student's life in the third dimension. All of the students who are at this point in the discourse are completely committed to ending the limitations of life in the third dimension.

It will mean different things for different students. The constant will be the discipline of the student to keep returning to the heart with the intent to LET THE MIND GO and to resurface only when THE MIND KNOWS WHAT THE HEART IS ASKING IT TO CREATE. The heart knows the truth. The heart knows your blueprint.

THE HEART WILL ASSIGN IT TO YOUR MIND TO SET FORTH THOSE FREQUENCIES. EMOTIONALIZE THOSE OUTCOMES SO THAT YOUR TRUTH WILL MANIFEST IN YOUR LIFE

Our students understand this in the deepest part of their being. This conversation would not be possible if students did not already have a clear understanding of this beyond their mind. So practice exercises that move you quickly beyond your mind. If it is taking longer than a few minutes, it is simply a lack of practice. Pick up the pace of your practice, and move yourself more quickly.

We recommend picking up speed at this time. There will be so many social, economic, and other changes in your third dimension that if you have not marked the mind off limits in the ways we have instructed, you will suffer nervous breakdowns.

We have witnessed this before. It has happened for millennia. Students were not prepared for their Ascension. We are here to assist in that preparation. Love yourself. Love your process. Love the parts of your mind you are declaring off limits. Hating those parts will not work. Loving those parts and leaving them alone will work. Love those parts, and when you find yourself deep in one of them, love yourself home. That will work.

The student is in charge of the pace and how long it takes to return to the heart. The student will decide to what extent she will practice the skills. Do not do this alone. We were not alone when we did this. As Mother Mary, as Mary Magdalene, as Jesus, we were not alone. Practice your practices alone frequently. That is mandatory. But create soul families, support systems and communities that hold you in their heart.

This is not a time for human beings to ascend alone. There have been times for that on your earthly plane. This is not that time. Seek and find support. Promise to call on each other when you witness those students trespassing into parts of their mind that are not in service of their heart. Hold each other to your hearts.

If there is conflict, there is too much mind and insufficient heart. This does not mean there will not be a need to confront ideas and belief systems. But let there be no conflict. Do not thrust your mind energetically at others if they do not agree. That is off limits. Simply breathe and move back into your heart.

Acknowledge from your heart the simple truth, "I hold you in love. I do not need to understand. I acknowledge that you are pure love and that is sufficient." When you say that or simply intend that silently to the other, it alters the space. Now there is a cocreative possibility that was not there before.

Cocreate with like-minded people. It becomes easier and easier as you acknowledge the unified field. Cocreate from the heart into the mind, and you will see that from understanding nothing you have gained everything.

BREATHE

DISCOURSE NINE

PRACTICE MASTERING DISCOMFORT

J: I'm feeling as though I should apologize to you. I know you don't need an apology. But I'm very aware that I need to spend more time with these teachings. A lot of what was showing up for me this week reflected the need to apply these teachings. I'm clear that I need to study them more and apply them.

M: Indeed. You have explained it perfectly. There is no need, of course, for any apology to anyone but yourself. For when you review the last dialogue, you see what you have done for yourself. You have created that trespassing that we discussed, and then you found yourself in the mess. You were awake and aware enough to say, "OK, I'm in the mess." That is preferable to being oblivious and in denial. It is more enlightened to wake up and acknowledge to yourself, "OK, I am in the mess."

So, indeed, that is the process. As you are learning, the process can be easier and go more quickly when you are engaging with others and aware that every unfoldment, every circumstance, every interaction is grist for the mill of the teaching.

We applaud you for choosing that insight, for you have chosen to end your relationship with duality by choosing to be in the insight versus in victimhood. You are choosing to enter into love, into self-love, into your growth, into the resonance of your spirituality, into your spiritual mission.

And, indeed, what is that mission? That mission will always be about expanding into more. By choosing to be awake enough to notice that you are getting messy, you demonstrate you have chosen expansion, Ascension, awakening, or whatever you choose to call it.

And beloved Joel, beloved students, this is the springboard for the topic for this discourse. For it is time to truly discuss the student's relationship with comfort at a whole other level. The discussion of comfort zones has been utilized before. Each student recognizes her own relationship with discomfort and comfort zones.

Here is the rub. Each student has an unconscious aspect of her mind that repels her from pushing the boundaries of her comfort zone. So the only way for the student to progress is to practice the art of integrating discomfort. Expanding consciousness involves growth, and GROWTH CREATES DISCOMFORT.

In the previous discourse, we mentioned that when students trespass, when they wake up to the fact that what they have been up to is not congruent with Ascension, it is very uncomfortable to discover that they are in the mess. This starts a whole other level of trespassing—shaming and judging themselves for being in the mess.

The only way to stay rational in the face of great discomfort is to learn to MASTER discomfort. When you study the practices that historically have been used to develop spiritual students, they always include practices to master discomfort by producing discomfort in the BODY—uncomfortable yoga poses, uncomfortable breath work, uncomfortable exercises.

Humans do not pleasure themselves into growth. Most spiritual students have difficulty remembering EVERYTHING IN LIFE IS A TEST FOR THE LESSONS YOU ARE HERE TO LEARN.

That is a beautiful paradigm. How fantastic for the students to realize that everything occurring in their life is a testing ground for the life lessons they are here to learn. Whether it is lack and limitation, whether it is suppressing communication, whether it is finding oneself upset over whatever is going on, these are the perfect lessons or tests for the student.

So instead of judging oneself for falling down, what if the interpretation was "Fantastic. I have fallen down, so I can use this situation as an OPPORTUNITY to get back to my heart." All of a sudden it is an opportunity, not a disaster. It is an *ah-ha* moment that fosters more growth. Who decides? The student, of course.

So the practices are NOT designed to be comfortable. The practices that we endorse—that the spiritual masters, the avatars of your third dimensional planet have always endorsed—involve MASTERY OF DISCOMFORT.

Perhaps it will help the students to realize why they hesitate so often to reach into their tool kit to practice a tool. They have not mastered the discomfort that occurs before the situation is resolved. What if not having it all resolved, just being in the chaos, was viewed as a perfect opportunity to master discomfort?

Many channeled teachings are coming through to humanity right now advising humans to change their lives; disrupt the status quo; end things that aren't working; begin things that the heart wants; say no to outside intruders; stay focused. These are all accurate teachings. Underneath all of them is the idea that the student must be able to hang out in the discomfort of not knowing. For that is what the discomfort is all about, is it not? "I do not know. I can't see. I don't understand. I don't like how it feels." All of this involves the fear of not knowing.

Now, beloved students, these are all products of the mind. And, of course, there is no knowing in the mind. The knowing is always in the heart. What if the doorway to your heart was actually paved with discomfort, and each state of discomfort was interpreted as one step closer to a full heart? Can you see how that instantly changes the entire paradigm? "Oh, this discomfort. If I practice correct consciousness with my discomfort, it will lead me to my heart."

Humans won't go to their heart without discomfort pushing them there. They will seek other avenues through the mind and through distractions. That is why people choose to live in ashrams and monasteries and rid themselves of distraction. It's much more challenging to stay on track with your mission while living among people who are living their regular lifestyles.

The students reading this handbook are living, breathing, and eating in their normal lives. Therefore, your capacity for discomfort, to have compassion for yourself when you are in the "I don't know part" must be substantial. How do you do that? It is much like a woman's body before giving birth for the first time. The body doesn't understand or know anything about that experience. Yet, when those contractions begin and the baby is being born, the body knows everything it needs to know.

Where is that for the student? In your heart. Your heart knows everything it needs to know. How will you get there? By developing an enormous compassion for yourself, accepting that the road is paved with discomfort. Why do you think austerity exists in the schools, the ashrams, the monasteries? Austerity is UNCOMFORTABLE. Indeed, this is the sign of mastery when students have developed such a tolerance, such a loving capacity, such a compassion for themselves with their discomfort that they LOVE THEMSELVES through it.

It is not about having lots of tools in the tool kit. It is about being willing to not know the outcome of reaching for the tools, to not know the answer and simply engage with the discomfort until it takes you back to your heart.

So if we use the example of your own planet as a model, it is easy to see the planet has been going through discomfort. It is obvious as she shifts and changes herself to her next highest order of integration. It is not about comfort. It is about moving. For transformation to occur, disruption must happen. The status quo must be changed. Full disruption must occur with regard to certain beliefs, certain brainwashing, certain erroneous assumptions about how it all works and, of course, that obsessive, addictive part that just needs to know the answers.

So for that realignment to take place, one must become much like a marathon runner regarding discomfort. The marathon runner may experience something called the "wall." When he hits the wall, he will know it because he has been told by his coaches and others that 100 percent of him will want to give up. All he can do is fight back with everything he has and continue moving his body forward.

Still, much like when women experience childbirth for the first time, there is no way they can conceive how much chaos it will produce in their body. And when they hit the wall, those that keep going are really just repeating one thing to themselves: keep going, keep going, keep going.

The purpose of developing a relationship with discomfort is not about asking the student to CHOOSE discomfort. It is to simply acknowledge that discomfort is REQUIRED on the way to growth. It is required. We have discussed before that the suffering one attaches to painful bodily sensations is entirely optional. There is no universal law that says when the intensity of pain builds to certain levels you must suffer. It is not law. It is a belief system, a very destructive belief system. Suffering is optional.

Suffering is the context in which that owner/occupant of the body is operating. The paradigm says intense pain equals suffering. The spiritual adept says intensity equals opportunity to become more expanded: "Let me go into this intensity. Let me use my tools. Let me honor this transformational moment within myself. And let me practice with this."

This is the way of the spiritual adept. This is the way of Ascension. It is the only way. The Two Marys definitely recommend developing more compassion for yourself and for your relationship with suffering. It is an option for you to simply choose to end your relationship with suffering, much like choosing to practice or to choose Ascension.

It is not true that one must suffer to ascend. It is true that one must CHANGE to ascend. It is true that one must GROW to ascend. And it is certainly true that to become a master, one must DEVELOP MASTERY WITH DISCOMFORT. It is not a fight that the ego wins. It is a giant SURRENDERING into the discomfort saying, "Yes, I embrace it. Yes, it is intense. Yes, God is intense. Yes, Ascension is intense."

It is very apparent that human beings are addicted to intensity through all their distractions—intense movies, books, and politics. Yet humanity has a complete aversion to FRUITFUL intensity in the body. "Let us make our women completely numb so they cannot feel their body giving birth." How does this serve spiritual unfoldment? It does not.

So to truly master discomfort, you must develop the courage to KEEP GOING. The courage of the universe is yours. How does God keep expanding? Through love, which is courage. Lots of injuries and hurts will occur, mostly self-inflicted, we might add, but it is absolutely guaranteed there will be injuries along the way. The adept says, "Goody, here we go again, time for more healing. Thank God I get to heal. Thank God I get to keep going with this. Thank God I have some idea of what this might be about."

It is such a pleasure for the part of us that remembers being human to witness the student's courage. It is time for everyone who reads this material to recognize that courage, to recognize that you already have compassion for yourself. It is time to turn that volume all the way up. It is time to say, "Yes, I will allow all the courage of the universe to be mine." It is time for the student to say, "I don't need to be confident about my ability. I can use God's confidence in me. It is not required that I suffer. It is only required that I SURRENDER WHEN I DISCOVER MYSELF SUFFERING."

SURRENDER AS FAST AS POSSIBLE. That is the mantra of the spiritual adept: "I surrender. In this moment I choose surrender." And then, of course, as the surrender occurs, the students are restored into that stillness, that purity of the heart, where once again they remember who they are. They remember God's love. They remember their birthright to be love, to be God experiencing God through this precious vehicle called a human body, to be loved and to love. In that place whatever is on purpose for that student to be revealed will be revealed.

So the consciousness of the student begins to draw on the God power of divine love when the student says, "I will redesign my contextual experience of living life so that I will begin to see everything that is unfolding for me as the PERFECT OPPORTUNITY—not some exasperating circumstance that makes no sense."

As that student begins that theme, she will be using everything from humor as a tool to exercises with breath, movement, and sound to discussions with like-minded individuals who can say, "Yes, I will hold the space for you so that your outcome will be fulfilling as you go through this. I will hold this space so that you will develop more self-love as you embrace your circumstance. And I observe for you and with you that because you are choosing to embrace this circumstance, your fulfillment will be deep and ecstatic."

That is how a soul family operates. Family members recognize that each one is in the perfect playing field for his lessons and that everything that is occurring is about those lessons. When the Two Marys walked on the Earth as women on a mission, they were exceedingly handicapped being women. Now in our expansion, of course, we understand how fabulous that we chose to be women walking with a Messiah.

How great that we could master our bodies so that we would completely understand our spiritual development from childbirth. We would then have the gift of being mothers letting our children break our hearts over and over and be women walking with an avatar that was at times loved and at times scorned. How perfect to master discomfort.

Now, students, look at your life anew and ask yourself, "How have I designed it perfectly to learn mastery with my body? Not that my body betrays me with injuries or diseases, but how have I actually set it up through those issues to potentially put myself in a position of mastery? Have I recognized that, or do I avert my inner vision from the simple truth that the lessons are showing me? Am I seeing it as a perfect masterpiece of creation? Am I able, even if it's painful, to chuckle and say, wow, I sure set that up well so I could learn more mastery. Fabulous.

"How interesting that my mind wants to run down that wretched track in my brain where the only possible outcome will be suffering. How interesting that I can observe that and practice not going down that path and just be uncomfortable and return to my center and say I love myself even when I'm uncomfortable. I love myself as God even when it's complete chaos in my body. I love myself no matter what I'm feeling."

It is time for the students to see the perfection of their creation in every domain of their life, in every circumstance. "How is this teaching me trust, self-love, courage, and compassion for myself?" Humans might think it is time to have more compassion for each other. That is not quite it. It is time for humans to have more compassion for THEMSELVES, which will then outpicture as more compassion for each other. But it must start with them.

Students, create an inventory for yourself in the different domains of your life. Are you aware of what lessons permeate every domain of your life? Is it courage? Is it compassion for yourself? Is it to have more trust in the chaos? What is the lesson you are currently experiencing? Start to proclaim your circumstances as perfect and be grateful for the lessons they are teaching you. You created them so you could test yourself, so you could learn your lessons. You are the master teacher.

The more you perceive, the more you gain detachment from the drama and the glamour of suffering. There is the belief in Western culture that it is somehow civilized to suffer. There is nothing civilized about suffering. If you are suffering, you are avoiding the lessons. You are avoiding practicing the tools from the tool kit, and you are being dishonest with yourself about universal law.

There is a term used in the human potential movement in your Western culture called "radical honesty." The Two Marys endorse the idea of radical honesty, which in an ashram, mystery school, or a temple the word *radical* would not be required. Every student would understand that the only honesty is full honesty. But in your current culture, you need a word such as *radical* because it is radical to be honest. Of course, it has become radical to tell the truth in your culture.

So we recommend a radical form of honesty for yourself, one that is tempered with great compassion because your culture fosters all this deceit, pretentiousness, and inauthenticity. As a result, being honest with yourself about what you are doing, what you are creating, what you are resisting, and what you are experiencing is radical. As you read this, let that be a little uncomfortable. There is a reason it is uncomfortable. Everyone reading this understands it is not wise or honorable to be dishonest with yourself. It is a habit, a learned behavior. It is not fact based, and it doesn't resonate with universal law. It is, in a bizarre way, an act of defiance.

So we recommend that you make an inventory of your life and map it out according to such categories as your relationships, your physical health and well-being, your spiritual life, and your money/material concerns. You really want compassionate, rigorous honesty in these areas.

How fantastic a cocreator you are that you have created these challenges in one or more of these categories at this time! Why? For the purpose of painting yourself into a corner so that you could transform yourself into something more. How glorious! What an artist you are! What a masterpiece you have created! Acknowledge that. Love that about yourself. Look and ask yourself, "How am I doing? Am I embracing each lesson showing up in each category of my life?" There is always one lesson that is dominating each domain. As you embrace that lesson, you will find yourself uplifted. You will find yourself refueled, for our Ascension Process takes fuel.

We recommend you do this process monthly. If you're truly interested in your progress, each year review all twelve months to see where you've been to acknowledge your progress and to consider where might you want to go next. What do you want to happen next? What is your life calling for next? Contemplate that.

The Two Marys wish to inform students that they may derive compassion from various sources that they may not have conscious contact with, such as compassion from the fifth dimension, their own spirit guides, angels and helpers; from the Christ Consciousness; from Gaia, who has gone before humanity and is actually in the leading edge of Ascension; from the compassion of nature; from the compassion of deceased spiritual masters; from the compassion of the animals. There is no end to the compassion available.

With radical honesty you will open yourself up to more and more compassion. At some point that compassion will move you to such depth that you will be permanently in touch with your spiritual destiny.

We want to acknowledge that no one reading this material gets sufficient acknowledgment for their courage, for their compassion, for their ability to surrender, for their ability to keep going when the going gets rough. So now at this time we offer you our benediction, our love, and our certainty that because you chose and you have been chosen, you are the way, you are the light, you are the truth, and you are the peace that surpasses all understanding.

If we were in front of you now in physical form, we would give you a standing ovation. Please give yourself a standing ovation on our behalf. We invite you at this time to stand up, to cheer out loud, to hug yourself, and to congratulate yourself for your part in God's plan, the Cosmic Consciousness, for your part in assisting in every aspect of the expansion. Thank yourself for showing up and receiving your good and your birthright.

You may call on us at any time to assist you in your grand adventure of Ascension. Call on your guides. Seek others who resonate with your plans for Ascension. Study the discourses. Have discussion groups about the discourses, if you choose. Practice your tools, and we will meet you beyond this dimension.

BREATHE

HELPFUL HINTS

1. CLEAR YOUR ENERGY FIELD: Stand and shake your hands briskly for about twenty seconds. Sweep your hands over your forehead to the back of your head. Then bring them from the back of your neck to the front of your body. Shake your hands a few more times, and sweep them down the front of your body. Hold your hands about three to four inches off your body. Do this to the back of your body as well. Repeat immediately and then several times a day. It will help clear negativity from your energy field and activate your chakras.

2. MEDIA: Turn the television off unless there is a program that is uplifting and congruent to your spiritual goals—perhaps a deeply empowering show on nature or an empowering story of a great leader who overcame huge obstacles on behalf of his mission. Those are great ways to resonate. Much of what is occurring in the media—on television, in newspapers, and in magazines— is so bent through the lines of force that it literally disrupts your energy field. It pulls you back into the mind. It shifts you from the pineal gland crown chakra activation into a hypothalamus-ruled being. The hypothalamus does not know true connectivity. The pineal gland does. So activities that disrupt the pineal must cease.

Therefore, turn your televisions off and select your news sources carefully.

Does this mean you are to have no idea what is happening on your planet? No, it means select your news from sources that are spiritually in tune because they deliver the information without anger, outrage, and making things wrong. Remember, everyone is participating in a collective agreement. Everyone chose this. Everyone has an opportunity to say, "I know the chaos is happening because it must happen. I do not have to thrust myself into the chaos. I can be spiritually enlightened with the chaos and find my resonance."

Receive information about what is happening on your globe from more neutral sources. Make sure that you are not engaging in duality and fostering more duality as you consult the media.

3. FOOD: Eat more raw food. When we walked on this planet, we did not cook our food unless it was meat. Most of our food was either fresh, raw, or sun dried, such as a grain made into unleavened bread.

Stop microwaving your food. This is an invention of the powers that are forcing the planet to stay unconscious. The science has been obliterated from your population, so the average person has no idea how harmful microwaves are, not only to their home environment but also to the very DNA of the food.

Start loving your food. Reintroduce blessing your food into your life. It does not have to be stilted or awkward. Simply gaze at your plate of food and say, "Thank you, I love you." And then begin your meal.

Rejoice while you eat. Make sure you are not in a negative mind-set or in a heated debate. When you proceed to eat, make sure you have cleared yourself from whatever might be upsetting you. That can be done very simply with a cycle of breathing exercises (following). Then bless your food and eat.

The human body is the most majestic portal and perfect vehicle for Ascension. Practice loving yourself, loving your food, and loving your meal in its entirety, from how you sit to how you eat. Chew, swallow, and breathe. Do not wash your meal down with liquids. Start BEING with your food.

4. BATHE: Take more baths and fewer showers. If you do not have a bathtub, fine. If you have a bathtub, we suggest you experiment with relaxing in your tub. Bathing allows you to be aware of, see, and love your body. As you observe your body, tell yourself, "I love my body." Practice breathing while you are in the tub observing your body.

The human embryo gestates suspended in salt water for nine months. That is the most primal support you will ever receive. It is more primal than your breath itself, for you did not breathe in the uterus. You simply sensed and felt. If you do not have a tub, we recommend immersing yourself in the ocean or find other ways to immerse yourself in water. When we walked on the Earth, this practice healed us from physical, mental, and emotional disease. Use sea salt or Epsom salt in your water. Examine ways you hide from yourself like taking brief showers with your eyes shut. That is not a formula for self-love. Taking baths can be.

5. READ UPLIFTING SPIRITUAL MATERIAL: We recommend *The Four Agreements* by Don Miguel Ruiz to support you on your path. Focus on the meaning of those Four Agreements in your life. You will see how they support and resonate with the teachings of *The Ascension Handbook*.

We recommend the book *Power Versus Force*, which explains the distinction between that which flows from spirit into a human's consciousness and that which is imposed by outside forces. Force is always of separation. Power is always of spirit. It will flesh out some of the teachings in *The Ascension Handbook* and help you recognize what is powerful versus what is forceful in your world and in your own behavior.

We recommend the works of Eckhart Tolle, specifically *The Power of Now*. If you look carefully at what is in *The Ascension Handbook*, 100 percent of the teachings are designed to assist you in being present. In presence the heart reigns supreme. The resonance of what Eckhart Tolle has created through his ability to calibrate himself in Ascension is most useful. Yet we want to remind you no outside reading is required for Ascension. What is necessary is practicing your tools.

6. PRACTICE BREATH WORK AND USE YOUR TOOLS: We have spoken many times on the power of breath. We recommend you find someone in your life with whom you can trade breath work.

We wish your experiences to be free from monetary exchanges whenever possible. The monetary system in your world is completely incongruent to divine nature and reality. It is far superior to exchange energies than to exchange money. Find someone with whom you resonate, who has read *The Ascension Handbook*. That person will understand and resonate with the power of breath work.

The frequency of these exchanges will be dictated by the level of intention that each of you has for your progress. Remember, your intention is not to show others how spiritual you are. Your intention is to be one with all, to serve God through your full self-expression. So exchange with others in conscious breath work where one coaches the other, and then reverse roles so that the one receiving gives back.

You don't need advanced training and expertise to coach someone in conscious breathing. The following simple exercise induces the pineal gland to release a chemical compound that expands consciousness.

It involves three cycles of breathing: (1) in the mouth out the mouth, (2) in the mouth out the nose, (3) in the nose out the nose, (4) in the nose out the mouth, (5) repeat in the mouth out the mouth and continue the cycle two more times. Support your partner in connecting the inhale to her exhale, continuing to breathe while she experiences herself in another dimension. Simply remind her to keep breathing. Hold the space of love and the knowledge that the breathing is enough. You may do this exercise by yourself, face to face with another, or on the phone with a friend.

For more advanced breath work, practice extended conscious breath work at least once a week. Combine the aforementioned exercise with full circular breathing for at least forty-five minutes. In circular breathing you connect the inhale to the exhale without pausing, as though you were creating a circle. It is best to do this with a partner who can simply remind you to keep breathing. If sensations become too intense, shift your breath into a shallow, light panting breath until that pattern integrates. Then resume a full breath.

The more you place yourselves in the state of expanded consciousness, the easier your Ascension Process becomes. The breath grounds you into your body. Your body is the portal for Ascension. Use your other tools as outlined in the discourses.

7. SLEEP: Make sure you have five to six uninterrupted hours of sleep every night. As we have mentioned, lines of force are pulling against your physical body. Everything from frequencies bombarding your body to the fallout from toxic discharges from jet planes to the toxicity in your food chain, your medications, your world of plastics—all contribute to the toxicity bombarding your body.

For the endocrine system to reset itself, you must have five to six uninterrupted hours of sleep every night. Regular exercise can help produce healthy sleep patterns. We recommend calcium and magnesium to help prepare your nervous system for sleep. If you have difficulty sleeping, we recommend a bath before bedtime with essential oils, such as lavender.

Ingest foods and supplements that help the endocrine system rebalance and rebuild. Eat raw foods, darken the room at night, and eliminate electronic devices from your bedroom. Consider using an instrument to produce white noise to block out city noises. Ask your guides to alert you when you do anything that might disrupt your sleep.

Remove caffeine from your diet if you have difficulty sleeping. Using caffeine to stay awake when you have difficulty sleeping is a form of self-destruction. It is also a way of denying your true feelings, particularly sadness, grief, depression, and fear. When you reduce or remove caffeine, pick up your tools to integrate some of the feelings and changes that occur.

End your day in the way we have outlined in the discourses.

8. RELATIONSHIPS: Evaluate who you are in relationship with and why. Evaluate the compassion in the relationship as well. If

you are the only one demonstrating compassion in the relationship, that is not a healthy relationship. Don't fight developing this awareness. Simply look at your resonance, look at what is in your heart and decide.

For example, if someone ridicules how you eat or that you enjoy taking baths and you have compassion for how you eat and bathe, perhaps this is not a healthy relationship. Recognize that everyone is not committed to the Ascension Process.

9. ASCENSION: You chose to ascend, and because you chose to ascend, you have been chosen. The entire fifth dimension and beyond are at your disposal. Will you utilize the fifth dimension, which loves you, which wants you to ascend, which has mastered Ascension for many, many lifetimes? Many of the fifth-dimensional entities reaching out to assist humanity have, indeed, been human. They understand what it's like. Will you call on them for help?

Will you remain open to the teachings of the fifth dimension? For they exist only for the purpose of Ascension. All the teaching from the fifth dimension is designed to assist in Ascension. The Two Marys do not have a monopoly on Ascension. The Two Marys have a frequency of compassion, direction, and assertion. We are not resonating only with the feminine energies. We are resonating with the ENTWINED frequencies of the masculine and feminine. As you ascend, you are not going to become more feminine. You are going to become more BALANCED.

There is always a need for the masculine directional energy. Your own desire for Ascension is a masculine directional frequency. You would not move if you did not have the desire for direction. So understand that the desire for DIRECTION is the purest expression of the masculine. The desire to CREATE is the feminine. These are your friends. Stay in that awareness as you pursue your Ascension Process. Stop looking outside of yourself for examples of this. You will have your own unique way of balancing this.

Students, you cannot return to the time when we walked on your planet. Do not wish for this. It is not appropriate. There are benefits today that will make it completely doable to Ascend. Do not wish for ancient times when the water was less polluted and the air was free of impurities. Rather, acknowledge that all of this is occurring now to build your awareness in a way that creates your desire to move quickly through the Ascension Process.

Stay in your breath. Stay in your body. As you use your tools, allow yourself to expand through your body into other dimensions. For those who are attempting to get out of their body, that is not Ascension. Ascension occurs THROUGH the body, through the gift of the breath, through the gift of life, through the gift of the resonance of the heart, which resides in the body and beyond.

Love your BODIES. Love your SELF. Love your ASCENSION PROCESS.

BREATHE

ABOUT THE AUTHORS

Jessie Keener

Jessie Keener is a co-founder of the Modern Day Mystery School in Ft. Lauderdale, FL. She is a naturopathic physician, workshop leader and breath coach. She has been a practitioner of metaphysics, natural healing and mind/body medicine for nearly three decades. Her metaphysical training and development includes using her gift as a conscious channel for fifth dimensional beings including the special integration of the energies of "the Two Marys," Mary Magdalene and Mother Mary. Jessie attended Mount Holyoke College and received her Doctor of Naturopathy degree from Clayton School of Natural Healing located in Birmingham, AL.

Joel Anastasi

Joel Anastasi has been a news reporter, magazine editor and management consultant. He is the author of The Second Coming, which records his interviews with the Archangel Gabriel through trance channel Robert Baker. He created a human development program called Life Mastery based on teachings from the Archangel Michael channeled though Jeff Fasano. Joel holds a BS degree in economics from Syracuse University and an MS degree from the Columbia Graduate School of Journalism.

LINKS

THE ANGEL NEWS NETWORK

www.theangelnewsnetwork.com

www.facebook.com/TheAngelNewsNetwork

THE MODERN DAY MYSTERY SCHOOL

www.themoderndaymysteryschool.com

www.facebook.com/themoderndaymysteryschool.com

THE SECOND COMING: ARCHANGEL GABRIEL PROCLAIMS A NEW AGE

by Joel D. Anastasi

www.gabrielsecondcoming.com

www.facebook/gabrielthesecondcoming.com

CPSIA information can be obtained
at www.ICGtesting.com
Printed in the USA
LVHW092154030621
689341LV00014B/263